The Economics and Political Economy of Transportation Security

TRANSPORT ECONOMICS, MANAGEMENT AND POLICY

Series Editor: Kenneth Button, *University Professor, School of Policy, Government and International Affairs, George Mason University, USA*

Transport is a critical input for economic development and for optimizing social and political interaction. Recent years have seen significant new developments in the way that transport is perceived by private industry and governments, and in the way academics look at it.

The aim of this series is to provide original material and up-to-date synthesis of the state of modern transport analysis. The coverage embraces all conventional modes of transport but also includes contributions from important related fields such as urban and regional planning and telecommunications where they interface with transport. The books draw from many disciplines and some cross disciplinary boundaries. They are concerned with economics, planning, sociology, geography, management science, psychology and public policy. They are intended to help improve the understanding of transport, the policy needs of the most economically advanced countries and the problems of resource-poor developing economies. The authors come from around the world and represent some of the outstanding young scholars as well as established names.

Titles in the series include:

Competition in the Railway Industry
An International Comparative Analysis
Edited by José A. Gómez-Ibáñez and Ginés de Rus

Globalized Freight Transport
Intermodality, E-Commerce, Logistics and Sustainability
Edited by Thomas R. Leinbach and Cristina Capineri

Decision-Making on Mega-Projects
Cost–Benefit Analysis, Planning and Innovation
Edited by Hugo Priemus, Bent Flyvbjerg and Bert van Wee

Port Privatisation
The Asia-Pacific Experience
Edited by James Reveley and Malcolm Tull

The Future of Intermodal Freight Transport
Operations, Design and Policy
Edited by Rob Konings, Hugo Priemus and Peter Nijkamp

North American Freight Transportation
The Road to Security and Prosperity
Mary R. Brooks

New Developments in Transport Planning
Advances in Dynamic Traffic Assignment
Edited by Chris M.J. Tampère, Francesco Viti and Lambertus H. (Ben) Immers

Transport and Ethics
Ethics and the Evaluation of Transport Policies and Projects
Bert van Wee

Institutional Reform of Air Navigation Service Providers
A Historical and Economic Perspective
Rui Neiva

The Economics and Political Economy of Transportation Security
Kenneth Button

The Economics and Political Economy of Transportation Security

Kenneth Button

University Professor, School of Policy, Government and International Affairs, George Mason University, USA

TRANSPORT ECONOMICS, MANAGEMENT AND POLICY

Edward Elgar
PUBLISHING

Cheltenham, UK • Northampton, MA, USA

Published by
Edward Elgar Publishing Limited
The Lypiatts
15 Lansdown Road
Cheltenham
Glos GL50 2JA
UK

Edward Elgar Publishing, Inc.
William Pratt House
9 Dewey Court
Northampton
Massachusetts 01060
USA

A catalogue record for this book
is available from the British Library

Library of Congress Control Number: 2015957861

This book is available electronically in the **Elgar**online
Economics subject collection
DOI 10.4337/9781785367779

MIX
Paper from
responsible sources
FSC
www.fsc.org
FSC® C013056

ISBN 978 1 84980 373 1 (cased)
ISBN 978 1 78536 777 9 (eBook)

Typeset by Servis Filmsetting Ltd, Stockport, Cheshire

Printed and bound in Great Britain by
TJ International Ltd, Padstow, Cornwall

Contents

Figures

Tables

Boxes

Preface

Security has always been a political, economic and social concern for society. Security, however, has many facets, and the public interest has varied over time regarding those interests that are to be given priority, and the ways to address the particular challenges associated with them. The events of 11 September 2001, involving large-scale assaults on the icons of United States commercial and military power and possibly of its political power, have led to a particular heightening of concern about the role of transportation, not only as a victim, but as a weapon to be used in terrorizing society. Since that time, little has occurred to abate this concern in the US and elsewhere.

The ability to attack the world's foremost economic and military power on its own territory focused the minds of other nations on their own vulnerability, although in many cases the long standing terrorist attacks of ETA in Spain and the IRA in the United Kingdom, together with the almost daily reports of bombings, shooting and kidnappings in developing economies, has meant the threat has never been that remote from the citizens of other nations. Security is not, though, purely a matter of terrorism at the macro, national level. Attacks within schools, cinemas and shopping malls have served as particularly poignant focal points for more micro concerns about individual security in places formerly thought to offer safe havens for the more vulnerable members of society, and for those going about their daily lives. There are also ongoing commercial concerns about the security of the supply chain in the face of acts of, for example, maritime piracy and attacks on oil pipelines that impose costs of an economic kind.

In this short book I seek to look at some of the important 'positive' and 'normative' economic factors that come into play when I consider how just one sector, transportation, needs to be treated in situations where there are concerns over possible terrorist attacks. While there has been a lot written about the nature of security and the best ways of seeking to ensure it, much of this has been focused on political, administrative and technical matters, and very little by comparison has appeared examining the economic aspects of security other than in the narrow considerations of the financial costs involved. Basically, accountancy calculations, rather than economic considerations, have effectively been at the core of this latter work.

The approach here can be seen, taken one way, as an examination of how the economic thinking of people like the Economics Nobel Prize recipient, Gary Becker, may be applied to transportation security. This entails bringing in more objective assessments of the ways individuals and organizations treat security matters, rather than viewing them as essentially emotional reactions to disruptions in society. But it also looks at questions of equity in protection as well as simple efficiency.

There are always thanks to be extended when writing a book. In this case the research assistance of Marc Tibault, Henry Vegas and Scott Talkington was invaluable in producing some of the earlier papers that underlie this publication. Over the years there were also many insightful conversations and collaborations with Mary Brooks, especially regarding maritime security matters. Many of the chapters had their origins in conference papers, and the discussions that took place around them resulted in considerable improvements, as did feedback on previously published material. Finally, money is important, and in this case support came at an early stage from a United States Department of Justice grant to the Critical Infrastructure Protection Project at George Mason University.

1. Introduction

They who would give up an essential liberty for temporary security, deserve neither liberty or security
Benjamin Franklin

1.1 BACKGROUND

Security is relative. No one can ever be completely secure all of the time, and when there is a high level of security the unexpected can easily change the situation. There are also various dimensions to security; are we talking about the statistical probability of being attacked, of having our property damaged, or having our livelihood taken away, or are we talking about feeling more secure, a matter of psychological well-being rather than of any stochastic notion of physical 'fortification'? At the other extreme of aggregation, is it national security that is at issue, or that of the individual, and taking a temporal perspective, is it the current generation we should be concerned with or should it be a longer-term view with a focus on future generations? But however security is viewed, some general trends seem to be widely accepted.

Whether the world today is a statistically more secure place than it was for our ancestors is a difficult thing to decide. Much depends on the perspective taken and, perhaps more importantly, on who you are and where. It is certainly much safer than in the very distant past when disease, famine and military conflicts regularly wiped out millions of people in a way that is difficult to comprehend today. Statistically it is also more secure than even a hundred or fifty years ago when much of the planet was engaged in world warfare.

Even with the current problems and fears of global wars, weapons of mass destruction and pandemics that confront us, we are probably, on average, more secure than during most periods of history. When compared to the position of a British 'Tommy' in the poppy fields of Flanders in 1916, a Jew in Nazi Germany, a combatant on the Eastern Front in 1944, a Chinese intellectual during the Cultural Revolution in China, or a Rwandan in 1994, the largest parts of the world seem awfully secure today.

It is also not only the direct threat of immediate physical attack that is important, there is also the indirect security that comes from knowing that kith and kin are secure, and that personal possessions are safe. From an economic perspective, while the loss of some personal items may not seem important in the larger scale of things, there is little incentive to produce and invest surpluses in societies where individuals see no, or at best minimal, benefit from their activities. For economic growth there has to be an accumulation of resources that the next generation can use to develop capital if subsistence is to be overcome.

It is no accident that economic growth in medieval Europe was 0.5 percent every decade; people had no incentive at a time of almost predictable regular pillage to produce surpluses. Planting and tending crops, and the construction of personal infrastructure, such as homes, requires time and effort and there is less reason to expend this if the fruits of the work are stolen or destroyed. The simple, almost rhetorical question is, 'why build factories or invest in equipment if they are to be confiscated or destroyed?'

Today, expectations in many parts of the world are different from those of our forefathers, and modern western democratic electorates throw out governments if their countries' gross domestic products do not regularly increase by 3 or 4 percent a year. This can even happen in centrally planned societies, although the process tends to be more dramatic and generally less frequent. But this expectation can only be met by meeting preconditions of perceived and actual security. Indeed, one of the main rationales for government highlighted by Adam Smith is the protection of citizens against losses from theft or violence of all kinds, although on most occasions this does come at other costs, such as the loss of some individual freedom. Like most things, there are opportunity costs involved.

Security has very many diverse aspects to it, and there are often clear differences between whether someone feels secure and their level of security from a purely actuarial perspective. Here the focus is on transportation security, and in particular the economic aspects of transportation security, and it tries to consider these two dimensions in the sense that security is what people think it is as much as what the statistics show it is.

Increased Concerns

For those living in the western democracies, and especially those on the North American continent, the latter part of the twentieth century was generally calm, with security viewed either very much a local issue of domestic crime, or seen as far distant, and often very abstract. The latter were seen more as threats involving national spheres of interests in other continents, rather than as imminent physical threats to the average person.

There were many challenges to security at a macroeconomic level in areas surrounding Western Europe as the Soviet system collapsed and nations like Yugoslavia broke up, but the threat to the security of those living in Western Europe was never serious. Within the European Union, there were certainly very many local difficulties, with terrorist attacks in the UK, France and in Spain towards the end of the century, for example, but these did not seem to pose a major threat to the broader fabric of society, or to the social order of these nations. Many countries in South America, parts of Asia, and Africa were less fortunate, with governments and governance often collapsing with a consequential decline in the security felt by their citizens. Civil wars were not uncommon, with the particular fears that accompany these.

The events of 11 September 2001 in the US proved something of a watershed in the public psyche, and have disrupted the feeling of security felt within American in particular, but also more widely in many of the more affluent nations. Indicative of this, even when there are accidents – a plane crash or a major railway derailment – increasingly one of the first things addressed by the media and authorities has become whether it was a 'terrorist incident'.

The fact that the attacks may be perpetrated by outside forces has had an even greater effect in the US, a country prone to isolationism, than events that are domestic in orientation, such as the Oklahoma bombings in 1995 that killed 168 people, or the mass shootings of students at the Virginia Polytechnic Institute and State University in 2007. That they may be indicative of a deep domestic malaise is largely ignored compared to threats from outside the country, and they are largely seen more as isolated incidents perpetrated by maladjusted individuals.

Looked at from another perspective, taken statistically, however tragic were the attacks and the extent of the untold misery they inflicted on kith and kin, the attacks on the World Trade Center and in Arlington in 2001 took relatively few lives compared to such everyday events as automobile accidents that produce some 33 000 deaths a year on America's roads, or the 11 078 firearm-related homicide deaths in the US in 2010. From a purely numerical perspective, therefore, terrorist attacks are only a very minor threat to life in countries such as the United States; they, however, impact severely on society's confidence.

Personal and public concerns extend across public safety and security; in fact, in many countries the same word is used for both, for example, *seguridad* in Spanish. Indeed, the distinction from an individual's perspective lies very much in the eye of the beholder. It matters, for example, very much who the perpetrators of acts are, the motivations involved and who are the victims. Perceptions and fears are also often quite distinct from likelihoods and events; many people have serious fears of flying but drive on what are manifestly much more dangerous highways with few worries. Globally, the actual number of airline passengers killed by deliberate acts of violence is small compared to those killed by truck bombs, but few think about their security when seeing a stationary truck close by.

Because, as we discuss in more detail later, security is a psychological thing, policies to enhance it involve actions affecting individuals' perceptions, often called 'citizen's subjective probabilities' in the academic literature, as much, if not more than the hard effectiveness of actions to stop terrorist attacks per se. Concerns over security basically affect the quality of life and this, in turn, influences feelings of well-being. In old-fashioned welfare economic terms, modern western society attaches a high level of utility to feeling safe and secure. As with health care, it is a superior good, the value of which rises with income. Equally, using an old-fashioned economic term, there are challenges in evaluating such an intangible feeling.

Security, as said before, always comes at a price; there is an inevitable opportunity cost. It is this that the purveyors of economic theory – the 'dismal science' – are beginning to highlight. These costs are diverse, and some can be expressed fairly easily in money terms, and others can be measured physically, as exemplified in the long lines at airports for security checks, the information needed to be transmitted prior to travel, the new forms of personal documentation that people need, the presence of armed guards, the searching of cargo containers, the checks before individuals can be employed, and the multiplicity of other actions that have been introduced or intensified since 2001.

Others are less tangible, such as the fear of public humiliation if found to be accidently carrying a water flask through an airport check. This is the price of reassurance, and hopefully of actual security. From an economic perspective, 'Who pays for these measures?', 'Are they good value for money?', 'What are the cost–benefits of various security options?' and so on are questions that are only slowly systematically beginning to be asked with some regularity.

Lack of Interest in the Economic Dimensions

There has been a steady flow of books and articles on security issues since 11 September, and university and professional courses have proliferated. Many have been in the form of knee-jerk reactions, looking for quick fixes to meet immediate concerns or, less positively, critical assessments of where security had broken down or seemed wasteful.

A lot of papers are legalist in approach, seeking legitimate judicial ways to ensure terrorists and their supporters are found, apprehended and dealt with in an acceptable legal framework, or that their sources of finance are choked off. Often there are international dimensions to this. Many actions have been centered on structural changes in the administration to enhance the coordination of security agencies and measures; the US federal authorities have initiated new institutions and helped reform existing multinational ones. Many offer technical solutions highlighting ways for detecting potential weapons, and most notably those that have become known as 'weapons of mass destruction', or consider ways of minimizing their impacts. Political tomes seeking diplomatic strategies and military adjustments to the newly insecure world have been published in significant numbers. Matters of ethics, and especially those concerning individual freedoms, have been widely discussed.

While many of these studies have focused on security in general, quite a number have taken transportation as their core subject matter, the theme of particular attention here.[1] Transportation modes have been a significant medium for terrorist activity. The attacks of 11 September 2001 made use of aircraft, and subsequent attacks on individuals using anthrax were executed through the United States postal system. Overseas, the US military had already been attacked by 2001 using bombs carried by trucks and boats, and the Japanese metro system had been the subject of a gas attack. The attacks in Paris on 15 November 2015 partly entailed shooting from cars, and automobiles were used to allow some terrorists to avoid immediate capture. It is, therefore, not surprising that transportation should be at the forefront of many people's thinking.

What has been largely absent from these debates is a significant body of popular, professional or academic literature looking at the particular economic dimensions involved. Certainly a number of books and articles have appeared focusing on some elements of this aspect of security, and in some of the other writings there are implicit economic considerations, but considering the direct financial burden of enhanced security measures and the even larger social costs, let alone the economic consequences of successful security breaches, there is a strange lack of interest.

The reasons for this neglect of economic considerations can only be speculated on. There is a natural instinct to want to 'win the war-on-terrorism' at any price and notions of value for money in security policy are thus redundant, or at least politicians are reluctant to refuse resources or to decline legislation involving any measures that seem to strengthen security. To some extent this separation between economics and security was most pronounced in the US during the presidency of Ronald Reagan when 'Reaganomics' sought to reduce civilian public expenditure that was seen as a drag on the economy but increased military expenditure in a Cold War offensive against the Soviet Union.

The issue of security is itself also not always easily amenable to conventional economic calculus; it is difficult for example to evaluate the success of many measures, and the full economic costs, outside of those directly related to the immediate manpower and equipment used, are particularly hard to assess. Compounding this, economics over the years has tended to become more technical and mathematical, and many of the theoretical models and statistical tools that have been developed, while potentially useful for looking at some aspects of security, are not immediately applicable to security at a sector level. The use of techniques such as cost–benefit analysis can, for example, offer insights, but they are limited, especially with regard to large-scale security initiatives.

With its increased adoption of abstract modeling, the analysis also tends to induce economists to focus on academic rigor and logic, and this is often at the expense of practicality or simply improving the situation rather than optimizing it.

In addition, by its nature security policy generally involves normative, as well as positive, analysis because of the need to target measures and to make judgments about moral issues; the controversial concept of 'profiling' as practiced by Israel is an example of an action that transcends simple notions of positive economics. This normative problem is not only about where to focus attention but also how to pay for it; some elements of security involve public goods, while others are not directly priced and financed from taxes. The burden of these monetary costs has to be borne somewhere in the economy.

The aim here is to fill some of the void not only by focusing on the simpler economic aspects of transportation security, but also in placing this study within a broader framework of political economics that allows security to be set in an institutional and political context. The book is not about abstract modeling, although deductive thinking is important for clarity and the odd equation is used, but rather the applied economics of the subject. It looks at what is going on, and its economic implications, as well as at ways of assessing alternative strategies.

It is set not only within both the narrower microeconomics of individual and corporate efficiency, but also within the larger trends that have occurred in economic policy-making. In particular, the past thirty years have seen tremendous changes in the ways society perceives economic regulation as market liberalization (to use the European term) or deregulation (if the more extreme vocabulary of the US is adopted) has been extensively pursued.

Transportation has almost universally been the subject of major reforms of this type. Much has been made of the more market driven policy approaches now seen within the industrial countries, but these pale, even if one includes the creation of the Single European Market in the 1990s, behind the changes in the ex-Soviet nations where state ownership has been rolled back and light-handed regulations imposed over what have otherwise become free markets. The privatizations and markets introduced into Chinese agriculture, however, are perhaps the most extensive of these moves of liberalization, and have had obvious implications for transportation. These trends are indicative of how economic policy has evolved, and inevitably are, perhaps not deliberately, influencing the way that transportation security is viewed and how associated policies can and have been implemented.

1.2 THE POSITION OF ECONOMICS

Economics in its modern form goes back to the work of Adam Smith in the late eighteenth century. It is a social science and thus directly concerned with the ways in which society functions and responds to different conditions. Smith himself, whilst extolling the virtues of free markets as the basis of a prosperous society, also spent time on defining the role of government and emphasized the need for good governance and security. In his *The Theory of Moral Sentiments* he even questions the social well-being that may arise from more efficient factories and management methods, and, in particular, raised issues surrounding the social pressures and personal damage that may accompany increased job specialization in manufacturing. Nevertheless much of mainstream economics since 1776 has focused on matters of maximizing the production of goods and services, generally measured in terms of gross national product, premised on a secure social system. The costs and other implications of providing this security, and the roles of the public and private sector have often received less attention.

Economics has broadened its scope in recent years, and especially since the impact of the Nobel Prize winner Gary Becker (1968) who began applying economic principle to a range of topics such as marriage, drug addiction, race discrimination and crime prevention, previously largely neglected. This trend has been reinforced by the creeping acceptance of institutional economics that essentially highlights the importance of context and transaction costs in the ways markets perform and the boundaries to market mechanisms. There has also been an upsurge in interest in what is sometimes called 'micro-micro economics' (Leibenstein, 1979). This is the study of individual firms' or managers' behavior as opposed to that of the business sector as a whole. In the security context, however, this focus remains limited (Frey, 2009).

Given these intellectual trends, it may perhaps be seen as surprising that economists have been almost conspicuous by their absence in the debates surrounding security issues since 2000. But absent they often have been. The annual meeting of the American Economics Association, the largest regular gathering of economists, has seen few papers on the subject and few in the selection that goes into the annual *Papers and Proceedings*: the paper by Cauley and Iksoon Im (1988) is an exception. There is little evidence that microeconomic considerations figure prominently in the thinking and actions of the US Department of Homeland Security, or indeed in comparable departments in other countries, other than in a very narrow budgetary sense.

In the particular context of transportation economics, there are virtually no papers that deal with security matters in the major academic outlets such as the *Journal of Transport Economics and Policy* and the *International Journal of Transport Economics*. Some papers, but still few, do appear on the topic in more general mode-specific journals such as *Maritime Policy and Management* and the *Journal of Air Transport Management*.[2] There is also an increasing number of specialized security journals that focus largely on matters of transportation security (including *Journal of Transportation Security* and *Journal of Transportation Safety and Security*) but the number of economics papers that have been published in these venues is comparatively small.

It is difficult to see why this should be the case. Economists have developed over the years a powerful portfolio of tools for handling trade-offs; indeed economists could be seen as the analysts of opportunity costs. For efficient use of resources, both between security measures and other outlays, and between the various security policy options, these tools would appear to offer useful guidelines, if not definitive answers, to the best deployment of resources and perhaps more often to ways of designing institutions so that such optimal deployments would emerge.

Not all aspects of economics have, however, been given short shrift in the policy-making processes. The development of a variety of quantitative techniques, combined with enhanced computer power, can also provide in a more tangible form some ideas of the costs of different system attacks and, *ipso facto* possible ranges for the effectiveness of policy actions. Game theory, although developed for a variety of purposes besides economics, is used extensively to assess potential outcomes of security actions, and the development of techniques of experimental economics offers a means of playing useful games. But to reemphasize, there has been comparative little done in this area and few efforts to apply some of the newer approaches to studying economics. In particular, the potential usefulness of the 'New Institutional Economics' to help understand the role of non-market allocation processes has been little explored in the security context, as has behavioral economics, under which some of the conventional paradigms of neoclassical ideas of utility maximization are modified. Oliver Williamson (2000) provides an excellent overview of this aspect of economics.

1.3 THE SUBSTANCE OF THE BOOK

The Boundaries of the Study

The aim of this book is not to provide a full blown theoretical treatment of the economics of security policy as it exists today and as it may be applied to transportation, and nor is it to take a completely normative view and critique of the more extensive work that has been done in what may loosely be called the political economy of security. The content of the book is much narrower and, even within its particular domain, is far from complete in its coverage. But it is intended to fit within a much larger framework of national security; transportation, after all, provides the lubricant for the modern economy.

National security considerations are multidimensional and inevitably involve trade-offs between where resources should be deployed and the forms and scale these resources take. But underlying these issues are policy decisions about which priorities should be pursued most urgently. Economics is basically about scarcity of resources and how best to allocate them for the public good; it would thus seem a logical approach to address many of the decisions that must be made regarding security matters. This inevitably has some purely technical dimension, but it is also an area that inevitably involves judgments about the concerns of citizens and what is practically possible given social and material constraints. Virtually everyone wants to feel secure, but most people are not willing to spend 12 hours at a time in a security line at an airport to ensure this.

The enactment of policy and its detailed forms, together with enforcement, can also be influenced by the voices and power of various interest and lobbying groups, and is certainly not independent of any recent attacks on society. We saw this in the particular emphasis on the aviation industry after the attacks in New York and Northern Virginia in 2001. But this is not strictly irrational because utility and welfare is about what people feel rather than some mechanistic concept of what they 'should' feel as if they were machines and just react as automatons, and with exact precision to some terrorist lever being pulled. They are not fully informed, base decisions on personal prior – and possibly strictly irrelevant – experiences, and have their own reference sets. The forming of coalitions of interests to argue a common cause is also part of traditional policy-making, and often acts to overcome rigidities when consensus is unobtainable, but also can result in policies in line with the views or interests of particular groups.

There are also formal institutional considerations concerning what can be done, the ways it can be done, and when it can be done, and these are influenced by the legal institutions in place and the associated governance structure. While they can be changed, this is often a slow process and essentially has to be taken as a given in the short term. Further, often superimposed over any notions of national security are those of wider international security and interests, which involve measures taken by nations and international organizations, such as the United Nations and the North Atlantic Treaty Organization, to ensure mutual survival and safety. These measures include military action and diplomatic agreements such as treaties and conventions. International and national security are, therefore, invariably linked, and thus inevitably involve interlinked economic considerations. This is becoming increasingly important in the transportation context, with, for example, international linked activities accounting for about 20 percent of the US economy, and with American citizens engaging in increasing amounts of foreign travel.

The Ordering of Things

Transportation is, therefore, only part of a large patchwork of considerations that those with responsibility for national and international security have to consider, but its characteristics generally place it high on the list of concerns. History also tells us that transportation is a disproportionate target for attacks; it is important, it is visible, it is almost ubiquitous, and its network nature makes it potentially vulnerable.

To consider the specifics of transportation security it is generally useful to have some understanding of the more generic ways that economists view security. In particular there are questions about the intrinsic nature of the product 'security', and where it fits within the range of goods and services that modern society buys and sells. In many ways security is like other commodities, there is a demand for it and there are those that supply it; but there are also some particular features that affect the way the market for security functions. There are also generic public policy aspects to security. There are, for example, matters of legal restraints on what can be done in the name of national security, a subject we offer only some broad comments on when relevant. But there are also more pragmatic matters of how effective various forms of public policy are, and in particular government interventions in markets, in combating perceived security breakdowns.

Since many security considerations are, by their nature, specific to particular industries, sectors or even firms, a number of 'case studies' are included that look at particular issues and policies. While there has been considerable attention focused on air transportation security, and especially so since the events in New York and Arlington in 2001, and on maritime security after the increase in acts of piracy off the African coast, although this has now abated somewhat, there are also lower profile concerns, such as with the security of shopping malls, major nodes in the supply chain, and recreational areas after the 2015 shootings from automobiles at Parisian café customers. Chapters are devoted to these sorts of cases. Matters to do with railways, public transit, and other forms of transportation are also touched upon when considered insightful, but are not at the core of the analysis.

What we do not do is spend very much time on security of the transportation of information, generally called cyber-security, other than in physical form, for example either as movement of individual expertise or documents. Ideally, we should consider cyber-security; it is basically a transportation matter. For example, it became a topic of interest for the UN body responsible for air transportation, the International Civil Aviation Organization, when at its Beijing Convention of 2010 its Security Panel recommended modifying its Articles to include acts to damage navigation facilities during flight. For an overview of some of the key links between logistics and cyber-security, see Transportation Research Board (2003) and for an assessment of the role of economics, see Anderson and Moore (2006).

One excuse for the omission of cyber-security is that of space constraints, as the subject is a large one, and another is a lack of expertise in the field on the part of the author. But more practically, the subject tends to be the domain of individuals outside of the traditional areas of transportation economics; namely communications experts. In many ways, however, the challenges are very similar, and the underlying economics are essentially the same. Having said that, there are important links between traditional notions of transportation and communications. Not least of these are the considerable information requirements of modern logistics; manipulation of these channels can potentially lead to as much disruption of the supply chain as a physical attack on its infrastructure. There are thus, inevitably, synergies between the secure movement of information and that of physical items.

The examples used in the book to illustrate, and the more rigorous academic work alluded to, tend to be mainly American. This is to a large degree because the US has expended considerable effort in enhancing its own security structure especially after the events of September 2001, and with this has come study and experience. There are also a large number of economists in America, and although relatively few specialize in the topic, this does provide the mass of analysis that has been completed. This does not mean that other parts of the world are entirely neglected but the coverage of the activities of other countries is more Spartan.

The book is thus inherently limited in very many ways, and what is not covered is probably more extensive than what is. There is little, for example, on the role of intelligence gathering, or on the financing of terrorism, the latter of which has become a matter of growing academic and practical interest. There is also little on what motivates people to breach security, other than to highlight in broad terms that motivations can be diverse, sometimes imprecise, and can change over time, making countermeasures difficult. Motivations are not always amenable to systematic analysis.

These, and other boundaries, should be very clear in the book, and to repeat, it is in no way meant to be a comprehensive study of security, but rather to provide some initial insights into the way economics may contribute to making transportation more secure. It draws upon many examples for illustration, although there may inevitably be better ones. It also seeks to take a balanced view; the objective is neither to praise nor condemn the efforts that have been made to make transportation secure. The task is not an easy one and it is, by its nature, not static. Rather we set out to show where economics may be useful, and inevitably in doing so, where it has been less helpful.

NOTES

1. Since 2008 there has been an academic journal dedicated to transportation security, the *Journal of Transportation Security*. While not a technology journal, in terms of what it does cover, the number and range of genuine economic papers is sparse.
2. As the former editor of this journal, I can say that the problem is simply a lack of submissions on this topic rather than a high rejection rate.

2. The scale and nature of the terrorist problem

The average man does not want to be free. He simply wants to be safe
H.L. Mencken

2.1 INTRODUCTION

Much of the concern with national security centers on ideas of protecting a country's 'critical' infrastructure, as well as on more immediate attacks on its citizens. The exact definition of what constitutes 'critical' is, however, unclear, as is that of 'infrastructure'. Both terms are also at times prone to various forms of political capture, although there is a general notion that critical infrastructure embraces the assets, systems and networks, whether physical or virtual, so vital to a nation that their incapacitation or destruction would have a debilitating effect on a nation's economic security, public health or safety.

More concretely, the US Critical Infrastructure Protection Board (CIPB) in 2003 defined critical infrastructure as, 'the physical and cyber assets of public and private institutions residing in the following sectors: agriculture, food, water, public health, emergency services, government, defense industrial base, information and telecommunications, energy, transportation, banking and finance, chemicals and hazardous materials, and postal and shipping'. The European Union's Commission has laid out the European Union's Programme for Critical Infrastructure Protection (EPCIP) in Directives (European Commission, 2006). Actions focus on infrastructure that, if disrupted or destroyed, would significantly affect two or more Member States or a single Member State if the critical infrastructure is located in another Member State. With due regard to existing Community competences, the responsibility for protecting national critical infrastructures falls on its owners/operators and on the Member States involved. How this is broken down into useful elements to be protected, or whether there is some sort of prioritization, is generally left vague on both sides of the Atlantic.

Here the focus is on one element of the American list, but one also implicit in the European Union approach, namely transportation. One cannot be too narrow, however, because inevitably efficient transportation often depends on the security of other elements; modern logistics and urban transportation systems would soon cease to function, for example, without energy and, as noted earlier, telecommunications. Additionally, the concept of critical infrastructure as put forward by the CIPB is a macro one, but there are also local, household and personal concerns over security that are very real if not of national interest in the larger context; others relate to individual sectors that, while not 'critical' to the national economy, nevertheless provide important social and commercial services at the local and regional levels.

Historically, security of transportation links and hubs has always posed challenges both to public and private sector providers, and to policymakers and regulators. Castles and redoubts have been used for centuries to protect key nodes in the transportation system, and particularly vulnerable parts of road, rail and waterway links. Convoys, caravans and other collective methods of protection have been a common response to attacks on transportation arteries themselves.

But putting some definite numerical or monetary values on the security threat and the expense of ameliorating it is almost impossible; the threat is often intangible, let alone quantifiable and so the amount of collective action is difficult to optimize. Waiting for a caravan to form costs a camel owner time and he must trade this off against the danger of going alone. A typical opportunity cost problem.

The best that is generally possible analytically is to provide a framework within which one can gain some insight into trends in the level of threat and its nature. History can help, local intelligence is useful, but they are usually just indicative by nature. The almost entirely subjective nature of the perception of any threat generally makes it distant from such things as actuarial-based statistical assessments that are often attempted.

What is often available is data on the number of prior incidents, the physical forms that they have taken, and their impacts in terms of those killed and injured, and the material damage done.[1] The availability of this sort of information is helped by the fact that those attacking the transportation system generally do so to be recognized and the attacks are thus high profile. The extent to which this type of hard data reflects the real threat to the transportation system can be questioned, and in particular the data tend to omit the more challenging task of quantifying potential threats or attacks that had been thwarted by the authorities. For example, six terrorist plots against US subway systems were exposed between September 2001 and January 2010 but assessing their economic impacts if they had been successful is essentially impossible.

2.2 THE NATURE OF TERRORISM

Terrorism has always existed (Parry, 1976), but while most of us have some idea of what terrorism is, it is difficult to define, and indeed the strict parameters of terrorism may shift over time as circumstances change. Some broad idea of what it is, however, is useful in developing the appropriate economic framework in which to model it, and for the development of policies that allow society to 'optimize' it in terms of transportation provision.

The term 'terrorism' comes from the Latin *terrere*, 'to frighten'. The *terror cimbricus* was a panic that occurred in Rome with the approach of the Cimbri tribe in 105BC. The French National Convention declared in September 1793 that 'terror is the order of the day', and the period 1793–94 is referred to as the *regime de la terreur*. Maximilien Robespierre proclaimed in 1794 that, 'Terror is nothing other than justice, prompt, severe, inflexible.' The Committee of Public Safety agents that enforced the policies of 'The Terror' were referred to as 'Terrorists'. The word 'terrorism' was first recorded in English-language dictionaries in 1798 as meaning 'systematic use of terror as a policy'. Although the Reign of Terror was imposed by the French government in modern times, 'terrorism' usually refers to the killing of innocents by a private group in such a way as to create a media spectacle. This meaning originated with Russian radicals in the 1870s. Sergey Nechayev, who founded People's Retribution (Народная расправа) in 1869, described himself as a 'terrorist'. German anarchist writer Johann Most helped popularize the modern sense of the word by dispensing 'advice for terrorists' in the 1880s.

A major problem in agreeing on a definition is that the word 'terrorism' is politically and emotionally charged, and this makes it difficult to provide a precise, objective definition. The contemporary label of 'terrorist' is also highly pejorative; it is a badge that denotes a lack of legitimacy and morality. Schmid and Jongman (1988) found 109 definitions of terrorism that covered 22 definitional elements. A study by Jeffrey Record (2003) for the US Army continues,

> Terrorism expert Walter Laqueur also has counted over 100 definitions and concludes that the 'only general characteristic generally agreed upon is that terrorism involves violence and the threat of violence.' Yet terrorism is hardly the only enterprise involving violence and the threat of violence. So does war, coercive diplomacy, and bar room brawls.

During the 1970s and 1980s, the United Nations' attempts to define the term failed mainly because of differences of opinion between members about the use of violence in the context of conflicts over national liberation and self-determination: essentially on what constitutes terrorism and what constitutes freedom fighting.

The modern definition of terrorism is thus inherently controversial. The use of violence for the achievement of political ends is, for example, common to state and non-state groups. The difficulty is in agreeing on a basis for determining when the use of violence (directed at whom, by whom, for what ends) is legitimate. The majority of definitions in use have been written by agencies directly associated with a government, and are therefore systematically biased to exclude governments from the definition. Some such definitions are so broad, like the UK Terrorism Act 2000, as to include the disruption of a computer system wherein no violence is intended or results.

The United Nations states that, 'The question of a definition of terrorism has haunted the debate among states for decades. A first attempt to arrive at an internationally acceptable definition was made under the League of Nations, but the convention drafted in 1937 never came into existence.' The UN Member States still have no agreed definition and this lack of agreement has been a major obstacle to meaningful international countermeasures.

2.3 THE PHYSICAL SCALE OF THE PROBLEM

Overall, the average scale of terrorist attacks is not large, but such attacks are generally focused and strategic in their timing and location. In the twenty-first century, attacks on air transportation perhaps attract the most public attention, just as the actions of Barbary Pirates dominated the media in the seventeenth century, although events such as the shootings in Paris in November 2015, are enhancing fears of urban terrorism. We cover air transportation in some detail later in the book, but one reason for this interest in aviation to be highlighted at the outset is the high visibility of the mode, and the geographical and temporal concentration of those killed or wounded. It is essentially a spectacle, and this provides perpetrators with the publicity that is often at the heart of terrorist attacks. Airplanes also, as seen in New York and Arlington in 2001, provide a powerful weapon of mass destruction in their own right because of the fuel they carry and their flexibility in operation, whereas most other modes are physically restrained by their tracks.

Attacks on Air Transportation

Table 2.1 provides details of some of the major attacks on airliners prior to September 2001, and as can be seen, the hijacking and sabotage of

Table 2.1 Some of the attacks on commercial airlines

Date	Place	Airline	Fatalities
Sabotage/Explosive Device			
03/28/1933	Dixmude, Belgium	Imperial Airways	15
05/07/1949	Sibuyan Sea, Philippines	Philippine Airlines	13
08/12/1952	Palmeria de Goias, Brazil	Trans Aero Nac.	24
11/01/1955	Longmont, CO	United Airlines	44
11/16/1959	Gulf of Mexico	National Airlines	40
05/10/1961	In Amenas, Libya	Air France	78
10/12/1967	Rhodes, Greece	British European Airways	66
12/22/1969	Nha Trang, Vietnam	Air Vietnam	10
01/26/1972	Hermsdorf, Czechoslovakia	JAT	27
03/19/1973	Ben Me Thout, South Vietnam	Air Vietnam	62
01/01/1976	Al Qaysumah, Saudi Arabia	Middle East Airlines	82
09/23/1983	Mina Jebel Ali, UAE	Gulf Air	112
05/03/1986	Colombo, Sri Lanka	Air Lanka	22
11/29/1987	Andaman Sea	Korean Airlines	115
12/21/1988	Lockerbie, Scotland	Pan American Airways	270
05/07/2002	Off Dalian, China	China Northern Airlines	112
08/24/2004	Rostov-on-Don, Russia	Sibir Airlines	46
Hijacking (resulting in fatalities)			
07/16/1948	Pacific Ocean	Cathay Pacific Airways	25
05/23/1976	Zamboanga, Philippines	Philippine Airlines	17
11/23/1996	Moroni, Comoros Islands	Ethiopian Airlines	127
09/11/2001	New York, NY	American Airlines	92/2750*
09/11/2001	New York, NY	United Airlines	65/2750*
09/11/2001	Arlington, VA	American Airlines	189
09/11/2001	Shanksville, PA	United Airlines	44
Pilots Shot by Passengers			
05/07/1964	San Ramon, CA	Pacific Airlines	44
12/04/1977	Kampung Ladang, Malaysia	Malaysian Airlines	100
12/07/1987	San Luis Obispo, CA	Pacific Southwest Airlines	43

Note: *Shows the split between airline passenger fatalities and those killed on the ground. The airline passengers are divided between the carriers involved but those on the ground are simply averaged.

commercial aircraft has a relatively long history. It also has come in a variety of forms with a marked shift away from hijacking in recent years as fear of the plane being used as a weapon has changed the response of passengers and airline crew from passive to active.[2]

Table 2.2 Some of the attacks on subways and trains (2005 to 2010)

Country	Attacks	Fatalities	Injuries	Hostages	Total victims
Algeria	4	0	3	0	3
Bangladesh	5	2	209	0	211
Brazil	1	0	0	0	0
Colombia	1	0	0	0	0
Congo	1	0	0	0	0
Egypt	1	0	0	0	0
Georgia	4	0	1	0	1
Greece	1	0	0	0	0
India	84	509	1517	3114	5140
Indonesia	1	0	12	0	12
Iraq	8	4	27	0	31
Myanmar	1	0	0	0	0
Nepal	2	0	30	0	30
Pakistan	21	19	218	0	237
Russia	24	83	282	0	365
Serbia & Montenegro	1	0	0	0	0
Spain	1	0	0	0	0
Sri Lanka	6	20	182	0	202
Thailand	25	11	62	0	73
Turkey	18	0	13	0	13
United Kingdom	2	52	701	0	753
Zimbabwe	1	0	5	0	5
Total	213	700	3262	3114	7076

Attacks on Rail Networks

Attacks on subways and trains are also numerous and are spread across a wide range of countries (see Table 2.2). Because of income and geography they appear more pronounced in lower income countries where rail passenger modes often form a large part of the transportation system. They are also generally an easier and larger numerical target for terrorists, the number of travelers by rail and subway being much larger than by air; in the US, there are some 4 billion subway/rail trips a year compared to 700 million by air. Put another way, there are fewer than 2 million airline passengers that fly each day, but 37 million rail and transit riders. There are also more points of attack in the rail and subway networks, and although missiles may be used to shoot down aircraft, the rail track network is much easier to sabotage, as was discovered in the two world wars. Further, the number of nodal points where passengers gather, and this says nothing of cargo, is much greater for rail than for air; focusing on longer distance travel, there are, for example, about 450 commercial airports in the United States compared to more than 500 Amtrak stations and the differential is more pronounced in most other countries.[3] Local subway and suburban rail systems have even more stations.

As well as stations and track, trains themselves have been attacked in a variety of ways. In 1995 there was, for example, an attack on a Tokyo subway by the Aum Shinrikyo sect using an impure form of sarin, in which 13 people died. The 2004 Madrid train bombings (known in Spain as 11-M) were nearly simultaneous, coordinated bombings against the Cercanías commuter train system of Madrid, on the morning of 11 March – three days before Spain's general elections. The explosions killed 191 people and injured more than 1800. More recently, on the 21 August 2015 three Americans helped thwart a terror attack by a Moroccan gunman on a high-speed train traveling from Amsterdam to Paris.

Attacks on Maritime Transportation

Seaborne piracy against transport vessels remains a significant issue that in financial terms alone was estimated in the early part of the twenty-first century to be costing globally in the order of $13 to $16 billion per year, although this has fallen somewhat since about 2010.

There have been particular problems in the waters between the Red Sea and Indian Ocean, off the Somali coast, and in the Strait of Malacca and Singapore, which are used by over 50000 commercial ships a year. Box 2.1 provides some examples. A surge in piracy off the Somali coast spurred a multinational effort led by the US to patrol the waters near the Horn of Africa. While ships off the coasts of North Africa, Iran and the Mediterranean Sea are still assailed by pirates, although at a greatly reduced rate in recent years due to international actions, the American Navy and the Coast Guard have nearly eradicated piracy in US waters and in the Caribbean Sea.

The International Maritime Bureau (IMB) maintains statistics regarding pirate attacks dating back to 1995 that indicate that hostage taking overwhelmingly dominates the types of violence against seafarers. For example in 2006, when there were 239 attacks, 77 crew members were kidnapped and 188 taken hostage but only 15 of the pirate attacks resulted in murder. In 2007 attacks rose by 10 percent to 263 and there was a 35 percent increase in attacks involving guns. Some 34 crew members were injured, compared to 17 in 2006.

Today's pirates favor small, fast boats and take advantage of the more limited number of crew members on modern cargo vessels. They also use

BOX 2.1 NOTABLE ACTS OF MODERN PIRACY

- During the 'Troubles' in Northern Ireland, two coastal ships were hijacked and sunk by the IRA between February 1981 and February 1982.
- In October 1985, cruise ship *Achille Lauro* was hijacked off Egypt by terrorists from the Palestine Liberation Organization demanding release of their operatives imprisoned in Israel. Following refusal, the disabled Jewish American tourist Leon Klinghoffer was killed.
- Collision of the *Ocean Blessing* and the hijacked tanker *Nagasaki Spirit* in the Strait of Malacca in September 1992, with the resulting fire killing all on the *Ocean Blessing*; two from the *Nagasaki Spirit* survived.
- Cargo ship *Chang Song* was taken over by pirates in the South China Sea in 1998, and the crew of 23 killed. The Chinese government arrested 38 pirates and executed their leader and 11 others.
- The American luxury liner *Seabourn Spirit* was attacked by pirates in November 2005 off the Somalian coast. There was one injury to a crew member: he was hit by shrapnel.
- Pirates boarded the Danish bulk carrier *Danica White* in June 2007 off Somalia. USS *Carter Hall* tried to rescue the crew but was unable to follow the ship into Somali waters.
- April 2008 pirates seized the French yacht *Le Ponant* and 30 crew off Somalia. The captives were released on payment of a ransom. The French military later captured some of the pirates.
- In 2008 the Ukrainian ship, MV *Faina*, containing an arms consignment for Kenya was taken by Somali pirates who demanded a $20 million ransom for the 20 crew members; shots were heard from the ship, supposedly because of a dispute between pirates who wanted to surrender and those who did not.
- In November 2008, Somali pirates seized the supertanker MV *Sirius Star* off Kenya. The ship was carrying around $100 million worth of oil and had a 25-man crew.
- The vessel *Ariella* was captured by Somali pirates in February 2010 but recaptured by NATO Danish Special Forces with the crew unharmed and the pirates escaping.
- Malaysian Navy SEALs stormed the Japanese-owned MV *Bunga Laurel* in January 2011, after pirates had boarded it. The pirates were captured with no hostages harmed.
- Tanker *Fairchem Bogey* was anchored at Salalah, Oman awaiting berthing and was hijacked in August 2011. This was the first time a ship was hijacked within a port's limits and taken away.
- Panama-flagged roll-on/roll-off vessel MV *Leila*, owned by a Dubai-based company, was captured in February 2012 in the approach to the Gulf of Aden. In March 2012 the pirates demanded a ransom of $2 million but the ship owners rejected payment. The vessel is being used as a pirate mothership.
- Somali pirates captured the Bolivia-flagged, Iranian-owned MV *Eglantine* in the Maldives' Exclusive Economic Zone in March 2012. The vessel was stormed and recaptured by Iranian commandos.
- In November 2012, a cruise-liner, *Azamara Journey*, was approached by pirates' skiffs off the coast of Oman. After making evasive maneuvers and firing flares, the pirates ceased attacking.

large, 'mother' vessels to act as bases to supply the smaller attack/boarding vessels. The points of attack are often selected when target vessels are not at full speed, making boarding easier. As maritime traffic has grown, many ships have to lower their cruising speeds to allow for navigation and traffic control, making them prime targets for piracy. Major shipping routes often take cargo vessels through narrow bodies of water, such as the Gulf of Aden and the Strait of Malacca, making them vulnerable to be overtaken and boarded by small motorboats. Other active areas include the South China Sea and the Niger Delta. There was also a tendency to adopt slower sailing speeds during the Great Recession to keep fuel costs down, but again increasing ship's vulnerabilities. Small pirate vessels are also capable of disguising themselves as fishing vessels or cargo vessels when not carrying out piracy in order to avoid or deceive inspectors.

Pipeline Attacks

Increasingly oil and other liquids are being transported by pipeline, and these have come under attack. The objectives in these actions are largely those of sabotage intending to cause economic disruption by reducing a country's ability to export, rather than to directly harm individuals. Refineries have been attacked for similar reasons, for example by the Islamic State of Iraq and Syria (ISIS) in the Middle East, although because they are large, relatively easy-to-protect facilities, this is less common than attacks on the extended pipeline networks.

Figure 2.1 provides some data on attacks on the Nigerian oil pipeline network. The pattern over time reflects a combination of the degree of terrorist activity in the country with the efforts of the government and oil companies to combat it.

Attacks using Cars and Trucks

Private cars and trucks have often been used to deliver explosive attacks (see Box 2.2). Car bombs can be seen as the remote descendants of the sixteenth-century Hellburners, explosive-loaded ships that were used to deadly effect by the besieged Dutch forces in Antwerp against the besieging Spanish. Though using a less refined technology, the basic principle of the Hellburner is similar to that of the car bomb. The first car bomb may have been the one used for the assassination attempt on Ottoman Sultan Abdul Hamid II in 1905 in Istanbul by Armenian separatists, under the command of Belgian anarchist Edward Jorris.

The attacks on restaurants in Paris in November 2015 also show the

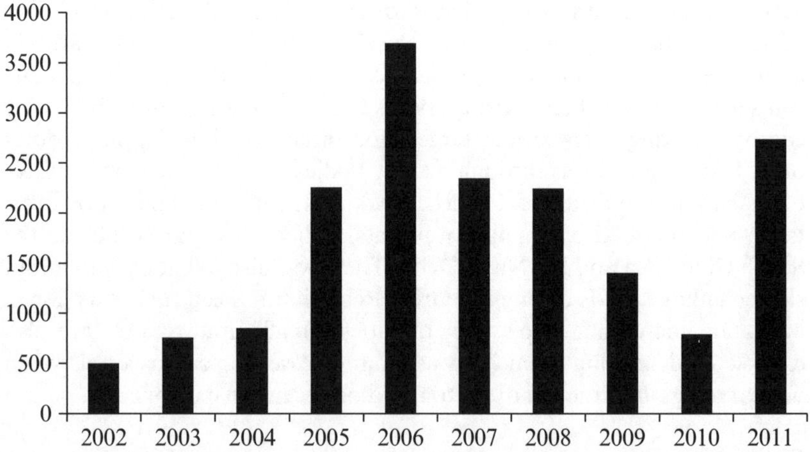

Source: Nigerian National Petroleum Corporation (2011), available at: http.//www.eia.gov/countries/cab.cfm?fips=NI.

Figure 2.1 Attacks on pipelines in Nigeria

potential use of automobiles as a mechanism for delivering local attacks using guns. Again, this is certainly not a new means of delivery – for example, it was a relatively common way for gangsters in America to terrorize neighborhoods in large cities in the 1930s and in October 2002 citizens of Maryland, Virginia, and Washington, DC were the subject of the 'Beltway sniper attacks' – but it has recently attracted more attention as softer targets are attacked.

The Hard Numbers

The lists and examples above provide some guidance as to the nature of terrorist and other attacks on, and using, the transportation sector, but they provide little guidance as to the relative scale of the problem compared to other types of fatality. Mueller and Stewart (2010) suggest that the dangers from terrorism are relatively few, or at least that they do not justify the economic resources that are devoted to combating them. Looking at some of the main terrorist incidents, they are compared in actuarial terms with other fatal risks. Some examples illustrate the point that they make. In the US, from 1986 it has generally been accepted that the probability of death from accidents at nuclear power stations should not exceed 1 in 2 million per year and 1 in 500000 from nuclear power plant operations; a review of

BOX 2.2 THE USE OF CAR AND TRUCK BOMBS

- In 1920, Italian anarchist Mario Buda parked his horse-drawn wagon filled with explosives near the corner of Wall and Broad Streets in New York City, directly across from JP Morgan Company. The explosion killed 38 and wounded 200.
- In 1927, Andrew Kehoe ignited dynamite and hundreds of pounds of pyrotol he had planted inside a school. As rescuers arrived at the school, Kehoe drove up and detonated a bomb inside his shrapnel-filled vehicle, killing himself and 44 others.
- In the late 1940s, the Zionist group Lehi used car and truck bombs against Palestinian and British targets as an attempt to end peace discussions.
- Viet Cong guerrillas used vehicle bombs at the end of the First Indochina War and throughout the Vietnam War.
- The Organisation de l'Armée Secrète used vehicle bombs at the end of the French rule in Algeria.
- The Sicilian Mafia used vehicle bombs to assassinate independent magistrates up to the early 1990s.
- The Irish Republican Army used car bombs frequently during its campaign during the Troubles in Northern Ireland and England. The Omagh bombing caused the most casualties in the Troubles from a single car bomb.
- Loyalist paramilitary organizations in Northern Ireland such as the Ulster Volunteer Force and Ulster Defence Association used car bombs against civilians in Northern Ireland and the Republic of Ireland. Bombs in Dublin and Monaghan caused the most casualties in a single day during the Troubles.
- During the Soviet–Afghan war, at a variety of training camps in the tribal areas of Pakistan, the Pakistani Inter-Services Intelligence with the aid of the US Central Intelligence Agency trained mujahadin in the preparation of car bombs.
- Agents of the Chilean intelligence agency DINA were convicted of using car bombs to assassinate Orlando Letelier and Carlos Prats, opponents of the regime of Augusto Pinochet.
- In the 1980s, the Latin American drug lord Pablo Escobar used vehicle bombs extensively against government forces and population centers in Latin America.
- In 1995, Timothy McVeigh detonated a Ryder box truck filled with an explosive mixture (fuel oil and fertilizer) in front of the Alfred P. Murrah Federal Building in Oklahoma City.
- In the late 1990s and early 2000s, vehicular explosives were used by Chechen nationalists against targets in Russia.

over 130 US federal regulations regarding atmospheric carcinogens shows that regulations came into effect after the probability of death exceeds 1 in 700 000; and a Supreme Court ruling in 1980 indicates that inhalation of gasoline vapors leading to a risk of death of 1 in 40 is unacceptable.

Table 2.3 Value of losses from major security and other incidents

Description	Cost
Estimated cost on the entire supply chain of a WMD shipped via container	$1 trillion
Cost of the 11 September attacks on the two World Trade Center buildings (direct and indirect)	$83 billion
Cost of cyber attacks against companies worldwide in 2003	$12.5 billion
Cost to the Canadian beef industry of a case of mad cow disease found in Alberta in 2003	$2.5 billion
Drop in the European Market (FTSE) immediately following the Madrid train bombings	$55 billion

Source: Eggers (2005).

Compared to these and other similar benchmarks, the annual risk of death from all forms of terrorism in the US between 1970 and 2007 was 1 in 7 000 000, in Canada it was 1 in 3 800 000 and in Great Britain, 1 in 5 200 000.

Of course these are aggregate figures with considerable variations around certain situations that make overall comparisons difficult. Acts of terrorism may, for example, be more common on transportation networks than elsewhere, thus pushing up the risk associated with travel. Further, the fatalities are deliberate acts of violence and this influences the way that society views them; society essentially seems to put a higher shadow price on a death due to terrorism than, say, a traffic accident. Indeed, agencies such as the US Department of Homeland Security place double the value of a life lost in a terrorist incident compared to a road accident. Given that the annual risk of dying in a fatal road accident in the US in 2008 was about 1 in 8000, however, this actually makes little difference in cost–benefit analysis calculations regarding where the highest returns can be gained from preventive expenditures.

Thus trying to put values on the diverse effects of an attack on the supply chain is full of challenges, some of which we will return to later. Table 2.3 however, provides one estimate of the costs of some of the major transportation incidents, together with some calculations of other major disruptive events.

2.4 MOTIVATIONS FOR TERRORISM

Traditionally most acts affecting security have been for direct personal gain or for the benefit of a third party. The person breaching security would accept a risk of failure and potential punishment for his or her acts, which may well involve death. This is a fairly conventional economic situation whereby the perpetrator weighs up the risks of failure against the rewards that may be earned. Basically he/she does a simple, often-intuitive benefit–cost calculation. The situation has changed in recent years with the person breaching security deliberately sacrificing him/herself; for example, this is the case of suicide bombers. The utility function of such individuals may be seen as reflecting the utility they gain from knowing that others will in some way benefit from their actions, the result of peer pressure, or that they themselves feel they will benefit in some future life.

Suicide attacks certainly date back to the 1660s, but may date back to the first century AD when the Jewish Sicarii sect are thought to have carried out such attacks against Hellenized Jews, and they traditionally had been made to inflict damage on the opposing side of a battle, or for political assassination. In many cases, they were not strictly suicide actions, but rather acts with a 'forlorn hope', with an extremely remote, but not zero, chance of survival if successful. In some cases they were also certainly designed not only to inflict casualties on rivals, but also to terrify them. They were not, however, often aimed at a more general terrorizing of the public.

In modern times the number of clearly identifiable attacks using suicide tactics has grown from an average of less than five a year in the 1980s to 180 per year between 2000 and 2005, and from 81 suicide attacks in 2001 to 460 in 2005. These attacks have been aimed at diverse military and civilian targets, including those in Sri Lanka, in Israel since April 1993, in Iraq since the United States-led invasion of that country in 2003, and in Pakistan and Afghanistan since 2005. These attacks have often simply involved an individual or group of individuals walking into a target area and either shooting those there or bombing it. But many have involved the use of motorized vehicles such as cars and trucks, and occasionally aircraft.

There can be issues in identifying if a bombing was in fact a suicide attack or if the death of the perpetrator was accidental, but this varies in different regions. For example, in some reports in Bangladesh, troops or police of the targeted state are the sole source for the allegation of a suicide bomber attack, and such eyewitness accounts can be unreliable. This issue of identifying whether an attack was suicidal is not such a problem in places like Israel, Gaza and the West Bank, where suicide bombing is an overt strategy against the Israelis that has the backing of both Hamas and Fatah. For example, between October 2000 and October 2006 there were 167 identified suicide bomber attacks, with 51 other types of suicide attack.

Suicide attacks are also a common feature of the situation in Iraq and Afghanistan and have been a tactic in Chechnya, first being used in the conflict in 2000 when a man and a woman drove a bomb-laden truck into a Russian army base in Alkhan-Kala. A number of suicide attacks have occurred in Russia as a result of the Chechen conflict, ranging from the Dubrovka Theatre siege in 2002 to the Beslan massacre in 2004. There have also been suicide attacks in Western Europe and the United States. The 11 September 2001 World Trade Center attacks are the best-known, killing nearly 3000 people in New York. An attack on buses in London on 7 July 2005 killed 52 people.

2.5 TRANSPORTATION'S VULNERABILITY

Transportation logistics has a long history, and in many ways can be seen as the adoption of transport economic principles within a larger supply chain concept. Definitions of what transport logistics entails are not always precise, but one useful idea put forward by Cooper et al. (1997) is that it is the 'relationship between transport and integrated approaches to logistics and supply chain management'. In other words it involves the movement of goods through the supply chain, but is more than just the freight transport aspect and embraces the full commercial and operational frameworks within which the movement of goods is planned, managed and finally carried out.

The modern, large-scale academic study of civilian transport logistics started around the early 1990s, when many of the current approaches were originally developed, but there was both an implicit interest in it going back centuries, and a more systematic study of military logistics from classical times.

Logistics has always been important for the military, and transporting men and equipment to the battle-front in a timely and coordinated fashion has since the time of Alexander the Great given armies a decided advantage. The advent of mechanized transport and of massive, often conscripted armies has made the task more complex but possibly also more important. One reason for the failure of the German Army to capture Paris in 1914, for example, was the inadequacy of transport logistics support; in effect it was physically impossible to move the number of men and their supplies through Northern France to conform with the needs of the Schlieffen Plan. It was also no accident that the subsequent stalemate on the Western Front evolved around two trunk railway systems – the German-controlled artery from Flanders through Lille and the Ardennes and the Allied one from the Channel ports via Amiens and Paris to

Lorraine. More recently, the overwhelming military success of Operation Desert Storm in 1990 was in part due to the transportation logistics skills of US General William Pagonis and his modern adoption of Alexander the Great's logistics approach.

More recently, the crucial role of logistics in the civilian sector has been recognized by the appointment of logistics experts to the boards of many major corporations; positions formerly largely reserved for financial, marketing and production executives. There are also many companies that specialize in transport logistics, in addition to the in-house divisions of companies, and in many cases this involves international activities as the 'global economy' grows and the supply chains grow longer and more complex. The educational establishment has also not been slow to recognize the modern role of logistics, and many of the prestige business schools around the world offer options in logistics as elements of their MBA and executive programs.

This change has come about for a variety of reasons; some are economic in their nature and others stem from the emergence of new technologies. Before looking at some of these in a little more detail, two overriding trends have been important in shaping the form of modern logistics. First, the length of freight hauls has increased due to wider and more extensive outsourcing and new approaches to centralization, inventory holding and terminal capacity. This means that production is now more transportation intensive. Second, there has been a 'time-compression' in production and distribution that has put pressures on the system for more rapid delivery of intermediate and final goods. This, in turn, has reduced inventory holdings, making the production chain more vulnerable to disruptions in the transportation system.

At the more meso-level, in terms of technology, the advent of the container in the 1960s, and the fact that Malcom McLean did not seek any patent on his invention, revolutionized the way that movement of semi-bulk cargoes could be conducted, reducing the costs of movement almost immediately. In 1983 US foreign ocean borne commerce was 694.4 million metric tons; ten years later, this had increased to 884.4. Ten years after that, it had magnified to 1167.9 million metric tons, nearly doubling in just 20 years. Growth of this magnitude is only physically possible through the use of containers.

The container not only cuts the costs of individual movements by a single mode of transport, but speeds up and cuts the cost on transshipment and consolidations between modes, making intermodal transportation a viable form of freight movement. Intermodal freight transport is movement of cargo in a container using multiple modes of transportation (rail, ship and truck) without any handling of the freight itself when changing modes. It also allows for easier handling of mixed types of cargo on a single mode – a container can have its own refrigeration unit or can be a 'tank' within a container-sized frame. The standardization of the unit being carried allows for economies of scale in the cost of manufacturing ships, wagons, loading/unloading equipment and so on. A container is also relatively easy to track, and can be sealed to enhance security.

The types of goods being carried have also changed, in part because of the availability of container transportation and on-vehicle storage facilities (for example refrigeration). There are now more high value, less bulky commodities being moved, and their origins and destinations are more dispersed than with most primary products. Their value means that holding large inventories can be costly and that there are often economies in minimizing warehousing and storage. Inventory management requires reliable delivery to ensure that goods and components are available at the right time and undamaged. 'Just-in-time production' requires complex logistics, including information systems, to ensure that the generalized cost of the supply chain is minimized.

The Logistics Supply Chain

Supply chains vary in their form and scale depending on factors such as whether they are domestic or international, involve perishable goods, are mainly bulk commodities, the costs of inventory holding, and whether special services are required, such as refrigeration. They can also vary by direction, for example involving the movement of bulk commodities in one direction and exotics, such as agricultural products, in the other. They are also frequently multimodal, often involving collection and delivery by one mode but trunk haul by another. In some cases there may be considerable interaction between the freight supply chain and passenger transportation; for example trucks and cars share road space, and many 'passenger' aircraft carry freight in their belly holds.

In terms of economics, the logistics supply chain may be thought of as a set of interdependent micro-markets, or in some cases a single market, for transportation services. Figure 2.2 provides a very simple illustration of the air cargo supply chain.

In depicting this, we assume that air is the chosen mode of transportation, which will itself be an economic decision; in some cases road or rail may also be an option, and in a few cases, maritime transportation. The shippers may either send goods directly through their own regional distribution centers, may engage an integrated carrier, such as UPS or Federal Express that offers door-to-door multimodal services, or they may go to a

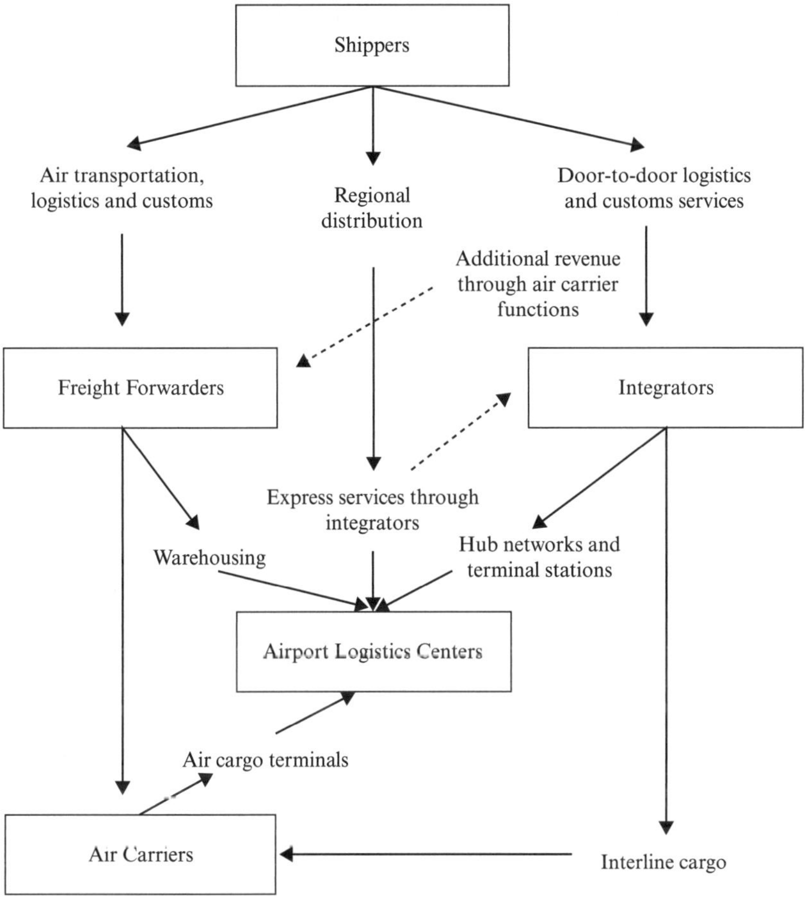

Source: Derived from Kasarda et al. (2004).

Figure 2.2 The air cargo supply chain

freight forwarder that basically offers wholesale services. The decision on the option to take is economic, and involves considering the generalized costs of the alternatives vis-à-vis their respective services. This is a market decision. But there are also sub-markets in the chain. While the shipper may select a particular airfreight forwarder, that forwarder will obtain capacity of air cargo carriers by bidding for space.

Looked at from the supply side, the various air cargo chains that coexist reflect the different business models that exist, which in turn can be explained in economic terms. Ronald Coase (1937), the Nobel Prize winning economist, many years ago, provided the classic economic reason for different types of industrial structure, and in particular why firms exist. The main reason stems from the existence of transaction costs. He argues that a firm's interactions within a market may not be under its control, but that the firm's internal allocation of resources is essentially institutionally planned by management. Consequently, as a generalization, the integrated suppliers that manage the chain internally cater mainly for small, lighter high value goods that require rapid and reliable service, whereas the use of forwarders reflects the need for less structured but cheaper services that are generally associated with moving more general cargoes.

Hazmat Issues

Some commodities moved are also hazardous – notably materials that are: radioactive, flammable, explosive, corrosive, oxidizing, asphyxiating, biohazardous, toxic, pathogenic, or allergenic – and command-and-control instruments involving routing, timing and packaging are often adopted to minimize any external costs of spillage (Hancock, 2001). This applies to cargoes carried by water, pipeline and air as well as road and rail. The amounts involved are quite large, about 10 percent of the ton-miles of freight movement carried out in the US. Table 2.4 offers some indication of the ways in which hazmat is moved. Such movements, of course, pose particularly attractive targets for terrorists because of the scale of the

Table 2.4 Amounts of hazardous goods moved in the United States (1997)

Mode	2002		2007	
	Thousand tons	Thousand ton-miles	Thousand tons	Thousand ton-miles
For-hire truck	449 503	65 112	495 007	63 298
Private truck	702 186	44 087	707 748	40 709
Rail	109 389	72 087	129 743	92 169
Water	228 197	70 649	149 794	37 064
Air (inc. truck and air)	64	85	*	*
Pipeline	661 390	*	628 905	*
Multiple modes	18 745	12 468	111 022	42 885
Other and unknown	14 241	2342	8489	1466

Note: *Estimates did not meet publication standard.

Source: US Department of Transportation, Bureau of Transportation Statistics (2010).

potential damage that may result from a relative small-scale attack on the supply chain.

Containerization

Producers use containers in increasingly integrated systems to move material and finished goods by all mechanical modes of transportation. A terrorist attack that utilizes shipping containers can, therefore, have significant consequences for the global supply chain in terms of pushing up the costs of distribution. A container-based terrorist attack can affect the container supply chain in four broad ways:

- Focusing initially on the maritime supply chain as an example, the threat of an attack that utilizes a maritime container in the short run could have the effect of dramatically slowing down the global supply chain. Even if the target container is isolated, government officials and private firms would be forced to check the integrity of all containers to verify they were not being used to launch additional terrorist attacks (Flynn, 2004). In the long run, nations and firms that do not provide acceptable levels of security would see a decline in the amount of containers they handle. This would have a corresponding effect on their economic well-being.
- Size is important for the economic vitality of ports and other logistic centers that handle containers. These distribution centers compete to be the largest and to have the greatest number of container-related services. Potential customers like the economies of scope that accompany this: they have a wide diversity of outlets from which to select container-related services. The larger the container distribution center, however, the greater the potential it has for becoming a terrorist target, and, because of its size and the greater the difficulty in finding a particular 'contaminated' container, the less easy it is to make it secure. This may lead to trade-offs in terms of size of container distribution centers, and the degree of confidence that customers have in them.
- Container distribution centers offer significant benefits to their customers and firms. If the activities of container distribution centers are disrupted as a result of the fear of terrorism then this will lead to a dispersion of container-related activities, and the loss of scope and density economics that accompany hub-and-spoke networks.
- Container distribution centers are not inexpensive to construct. They also have significant concentrations of capital machinery. Thus any terrorist attack that inflicts serious damage on a container

distribution center will result in significant costs being added to the value chain. These costs may not be large in global terms, but they will have implications for the relative attractiveness of different centers and thus will have impacts on the spatial distribution of containers.

2.6 SOME GENERAL OBSERVATIONS

Transportation and supply chain security is multifaceted, and has been so throughout history. The nature of the threats posed has obviously changed with time as transportation technology and life styles have evolved, and as the scale of the threat has fluctuated along with the motivations of those posing it. This complexity of interactions between causes and effects continues today, and the threats posed vary by geography and attacks by methods of execution and severity. All of this leads to the heterogeneity of the security threats posed for transportation suppliers and users, and with this their response functions, and those of government.

There is, however, a certain amount of 'fashion' involved in what we see in the short term, with such things as piracy being in vogue for a time, hijacks of planes at other times, and car bombing at others. This may be due to a sort of copycat mentality on the part of perpetrators, or because of the nature of the underlying motivations, or because relative prevention techniques have changed. The duration of any fashion would seem to some extent to depend upon the successes achieved or the ability of the security agencies or private companies to combat the attacks.

Fashion in terms of the modes attacked also seems to vary over time with a marked diminution in aircraft attacks since the early 2000s, but a period of increase in maritime piracy, at least until recently, and the use of motor vehicles as the means of delivery. Again this may be related to the underlying motivations of perpetrators and the reactions of the authorities, but the nature of the local transportation systems and the degree of any mode's vulnerability is also likely to play an important role. But certainly, the range and forms of attack have varied considerably over time and are likely to continue to vary in the future.

NOTES

1. The National Counterterrorism Center incident data provides statistics on terrorist activities around the globe; see http://www.nctc.gov/site/other/wits.html.

2. The economic treatment of the pre-terrorist phase of hijacking was much more in terms of traditional neoclassical economics; see Landes (1978).
3. Brian Jenkins, of the Mineta Transportation Institute was quoted in *USA Today* (28 December 2010), 'One hundred percent screening of rail passengers is not realistic. You might need hundreds of thousands of screeners'. He went on to estimate that it would cost $8 to $10 to screen each passenger.

3. Some basic economics of transportation security

Uncertainty is the only certainty there is, and knowing how to live with insecurity is the only security
John Allen Paulos

The user's going to pick dancing pigs over security every time
Bruce Schneier

3.1 INTRODUCTION

Much of the public reaction in the United States, and that of the public authorities, to the 2001 attacks on New York and Northern Virginia was essentially a knee-jerk. Politicians felt that something should be done to maintain public confidence, and almost any sort of action was a natural recourse. The issue was as much one of assuring public confidence as it was of preventing further acts of terrorism. There was an inevitable feeling that inertia in these circumstances would be perceived to be a sign of weakness, and lack of command of the situation. Almost any action was thus seen as important in maintaining public confidence.

There are, however, opportunity costs inherent in this, and gradually this has been explicitly recognized. The longer-term approach has been more measured, and involved significant broader national and international institutional changes in addition to the deployment of explicit anti-terrorist measures at the micro, generally local jurisdiction level. The creation of the Transportation Security Administration (TSA) in 2001 and its subsequent embedding in the Department of Homeland Security is perhaps the most obvious transportation manifestation of this at the national level, with actions at such bodies as the International Maritime Organization and International Civil Aviation Organization reflecting international initiatives.

This sort of situation applies to any other sector of the economy, and not just aviation, which was immediately impacted after 11 September, or even transportation more generally, although we focus on the transport sector. The full economic implications stemming from the revised security measures that have emerged for air transportation, transit systems, shipping, trucking and other transportation industries as a result of the response to the event of 2001, are still imperfectly understood from an intellectual standpoint, and quantification of the key economic parameters by the authorities remains primitive, if there is any attempt at this at all. In simple terms we have little idea of what the benefits of these measures have been regarding reducing the risks of attack, or of the costs on the economy of enacting the portfolio of laws and regulations that are now in place. As a chief economist at the Department of Homeland Security once put it, 'We really don't know a whole lot about the overall costs and benefits of homeland security.' (Anderson, 2006).

This leaves a whole slew of both technical, positive economics and political economy issues to address, not least because it is the government that ultimately influences the allocation of resources, be it those directly under its own control or those in private hands that it can direct by laws and regulations.[1] Even markets operate within institutional frameworks established by government and operated with a governance structure. Prioritizing what to do, therefore, is often not simply a matter of conventional economic efficiency considerations, even if efficiency could be quantified. There are the issues of public perception and understanding, both of threats and of the ways in which they are being handled. There are also issues of equity – how security measures will affect various groups in society, including those that are not yet born, and who is to pay the costs of their implementation. This inter-temporal problem is effectively the age-old one of how many members of a village should tend the fields, and directly produce food, and how many should stand guard to protect the farmers. The latter group reduces immediate output, but may add to longer-term production by reducing risks of losses from attacks and pillaging.

In the specific context of transportation, its services are demanded not in their own right but because of the benefits they confer in terms of the production of final goods and services; they meet a 'derived demand'. People regularly complain about the discomforts of modern flying, but enjoy the results when they reach their destinations. Transportation is also a network industry consisting of numerous competing and complementing nodes and links that take a diversity of forms. This leaves it relatively exposed, as we saw in Chapter 2, either as movement is taking place, for example on buses or trains, or where people or goods are being gathered for transportation, for example at bus terminals, airports and railroad stations.[2]

Economies of scale, scope and density in the provision of transportation services also mean that from a commercial perspective there are often efficiency gains associated with concentrating traffic. This is the primary rationale behind the hub-and-spoke configuration of services offered by many transport service providers – in the case of air travelers, passengers from small cities are funneled through large hub airports where they change planes for their final destinations. It also explains why transportation takes place along corridors, even when a more scattered pattern of movement is physically possible.

3.2 SIZE AND NATURE OF THE TRANSPORTATION SECTOR

The Macroeconomic Importance of Transportation

Transportation is unquestionably important, and has been since mankind appeared. It acts as the lubricant that allows individuals to go about their everyday activities, and for firms to bring together land, labor and capital to produce the goods and services upon which society depends. The aim here is certainly not to try to paint a full picture of the role and importance of modern transportation but rather to provide a little background to illustrate what we would lose if there were severe restrictions, either because of the damage done by terrorist attacks or from the burden of extensive measures to reduce these attacks, placed upon the ways in which transportation services can be delivered. The arguments and the issues apply to varying degrees to all levels of transportation, be it regional or international in its orientation, although we focus on the larger picture.

We begin by looking at international trade flows that transportation facilitates. While there are cycles in trade associated with the state of the global economy, in 2012 there was $36 534 billion worth of recorded trade conducted across international borders, and no doubt there was much more that fell out of the official statistics. While much of this involved the traditional industrial regions such as Europe ($4468.6 billion, of which $2575.7 billion involved Germany), the United States ($3882.4 billion), and Japan ($1684.4), the new mega-economy of China ($3866.9 billion) is also now a major player.

A large part of this international trade involves the physical movement of raw material and final goods, but there have been important changes in the nature of trade as more service-oriented economies have emerged, and the weight/value of many items traded has fallen significantly. This affects the transportation inputs into trade, with an increasing emphasis being placed on the speed and reliability of services rather than just the simple monetary costs. For example, while international shipping carriers handled some 90 percent of global trade measured by weight, air transportation accounts for something of the order of 40 percent of trade by value, despite only handling 195.4 billion revenue tonne-kilometers in 2011; shipping handled about 70 500 billion tonne-kilometers in 2012 by way of comparison.[3]

Road and rail also play an important role in international trade, as well as being the dominant modes for domestic transportation in most countries, and most obviously for those that are landlocked. But even in a country such as the United States, with large amounts of coastline and seaports, land modes carry a significant part of the international transportation trade flow (Table 3.1).

Unlike air and sea transportation, where there are certainly air- and sea-lanes defined by statute, land-based modes require the provision of physical track as well as terminals. As a generalization, transportation infrastructure is physically large, and inevitably expensive, and that generally

Table 3.1 Value of US merchandise trade by land, water and air gateways: 1990–2008 (current $ billion)

Year	US international merchandise trade	US land trade	US water trade	US air trade
1990	889	204	434	201
1991	910	210	435	209
1992	981	232	463	226
1993	1046	258	477	255
1994	1176	312	517	293
1995	1328	338	573	355
1996	1420	377	591	382
1997	1559	426	626	433
1998	1594	452	614	442
1999	1720	501	632	496
2000	2000	576	740	593
2001	1870	547	718	519
2002	1854	541	729	498
2003	1982	563	811	523
2004	2288	634	959	599
2005	2579	698	1122	652
2006	2891	760	1279	731
2007	3119	797	1399	781
2008	3401	830	1624	806

Source: US Department of Transportation, Bureau of Transportation Statistics (2009), *America's Freight Transportation Gateways: Connecting our Nation to Places and Markets Abroad*, Washington, DC: USDOT.

entails immobile investments that seldom have uses beyond those they were designed for – in economic terms the vast majority of such infrastructure can be seen as a 'sunk cost'. But, while it often has very few alternative uses, its generally specific nature also often makes it difficult to find good alternatives should it be destroyed, and replacement can be costly and take time.

While it is not always easy to separate international from domestic air and sea transportation – several major United States hub airports, for example, serve both roles – the distinction is even less clear for road and rail infrastructure. In addition, land modes play a major network role in international trade not only as a significant cross-border mode in their own right, but also in providing feeder services to sea and air movements.

The Microeconomic Importance of Transportation

The lapses in security that attract most media attention, while local in their immediate impact, can ultimately do damage to the macroeconomic or political system. While in aggregate the importance of transportation to a national economy and to international trade, and *ipso facto* as a target for attack, is fairly easy to see, there are more micro issues concerning the everyday life of individuals. People use transportation to go to work, to visit family and friends, and to enjoy leisure pursuits. Given the large number of individual movements involved, attacks on transportation networks are seldom designed to interfere directly with individuals' travels, but rather to make transportation as a whole less convenient and more costly, and to make society as a collective feel unsafe in pursuing its normal activities.

But there is also a more micro aspect to transportation. Most personal trips are relatively short and, given the increases in urbanization, made in cities. Globally, the majority of trips are on foot or by bicycle, and direct attacks on individuals are in these cases mainly to commit crimes of robbery or common assault, rather than having any underlying terrorist motivation. The more prevalent attacks by terrorists at the micro level involve motorized transportation used by groups of individuals, namely buses, trams and trains. Attacks on these local networks are relatively easy and cheap, but preventing them is difficult and resource-intensive.

In terms of the composition and importance of these local networks, much depends on the area involved and the prosperity of the population. Cities require networks of roads and various forms of railway to allow their populations and businesses the mobility required to ensure efficient production and to offer citizens a reasonable level of social interaction. On these roads and tracks run millions of cars, buses, trams and suburban trains in addition to pedestrians, cyclists and, in lower income countries, 'beasts of burden', and added to this are the trucks and vans doing pick-ups and collections.

While aggregate figures are not always helpful in this context, some idea of the importance of local, microeconomic systems can be gleaned from the fact that the world's car park reached one billion vehicles in 2010 with rapid growth in the large emerging economies such as China. Local variations in ownership, as well as vehicle use, are considerable but often difficult to quantify in detail. At the national level, data from the World Bank shows that in 2010 car ownership levels range from 1263 per 1000 population in San Marino, and 797 in the US, to 5 in Rwanda and 3 in Bangladesh, but how accurate these figures are in the poorer countries is almost guesswork.

Urban public transportation, a common target for bombings, shooting and, in the case of the attack on the Japanese metro system in 1995, gas attacks, is varied in both its nature and its coverage. Some of the metro systems are extremely large – for example, the New York subway has 842 miles of track and in 2012 delivered 1.65 billion rides; the Tokyo subway caters for 8.7 million daily passengers (although this only represents 22 percent of Tokyo's 40 million daily rail passengers), and Moscow's Metro averages about 6.73 million passenger a day – and any serious disruption to them has major social and economic implications for the area involved, as well as being potentially costly to repair.

In addition to mechanized transportation – cars, buses and trains – local transportation involves considerable walking, and in some cities cycling. The exact numbers are impossible to calculate, but this 'human' mode is essentially for short trips at the microeconomic level, especially in low-income countries where alternatives are too expensive. Pedestrians have been a common target for attacks in many countries, both by muggers and thieves, but also terrorists and kidnappers, largely because of the near impossibility of offering them full protection.

3.3 WIDER REASONS FOR TRANSPORTATION BEING A TARGET

As the Swiss economist, Bruno Frey (2009), has pointed out terrorists are rational in their behavior, they want to achieve their goals at minimum cost, and they seek efficiency. The goals themselves may be difficult for the non-terrorist to comprehend, but from an economic perspective this is not the issue other than that they exist. The terrorists will, therefore, seek targets that meet certain criteria, and in particular will be likely to attack those formations of transportation with at least some of the following characteristics:

- high visibility so as to attract the maximum media and government attention;
- that will cause immediate disruption to the economic system, and particularly to the wider economic structure of the economy, so as to impact on the physical well-being of a large population;
- soft targets that are difficult to protect and allow terrorists easy access but relatively straightforward to damage;
- linked in some way to the government, either directly or indirectly as, say, subcontractors, so as to impede efficient governance and cast doubt over the authorities' own abilities to protect themselves.

Many elements of transportation meet all these criteria to a greater or lesser degree. In addition to the major role that transportation fulfills in a modern economy, the media and public attention that events like airliner or rail crashes attract highlights the potential physiological impact of a successful terrorist attack, or even a failed one. Transportation, because of its extensive infrastructure, large terminals, and numerous operating units, makes it relatively easy to penetrate, and provides scope for introducing relatively large pieces of destructive hardware. In addition, transportation in all countries involves massive amounts of direct public investment and various forms of what may conveniently be called public/private activities. Terrorist attacks may thus be marketed by perpetrators as aimed at the 'State' rather than random individuals or businesses; the latter being treated by terrorists as collateral damage. The very decentralization of transportation, coupled with high visibility and its economic connectivity, makes it vulnerable to attack and an attractive target.

3.4 RISK AND UNCERTAINTY

Transportation is subject to both risk and uncertainty in terms of its security. This raises linked issues about the nature of safety and security. While there is a linguistic commonality between the terms 'safety' and 'security' in some languages, they are in practice treated rather differently by economists, and indeed, often in the ways in which policy-makers handle them.[4]

The Distinction

At the outset it is, therefore, useful to clarify elements of the terminology used in the security arena to gain a foothold on some of the economic nuances involved in security matters. A particular problem is that there are issues of both risk and uncertainty to be considered when examining the policy issue of any forms of security.[5] The conceptual distinction between risk and uncertainty was initially drawn by the American economist Frank Knight (1921) over 90 years ago, and although somewhat imprecise when it comes to calculations, it offers a helpful dichotomy.

In our context, there is initially the matter of separating out pure risk, which has more to do with transportation safety and with what are conventionally seen as criminal acts such as theft and personal assaults, and pure uncertainty, which is more to do with terrorism. Each has its own impacts on society, and public policy responses usually need to differ to handle them with any degree of success.

Put simply, risk has a statistical probability associated with it while uncertainty does not. Such probabilities exist because the acts involved are frequent, and fairly clearly defined, allowing the law of large numbers to be invoked. For example, if it is observed that in the past young adult male drivers have a minor accident on average every 120000 miles they drive, one can estimate a risk factor for this group of drivers. This means that under most circumstances it should be possible to insure against risk but this is not so with uncertainty where there is no known probability. Indeed, this is exactly what actuaries do and how insurance premiums are calculated, they are based on calculated level of risk. The premiums may be lower for young female drivers if they on average only have accidents, say, every 150000 miles driven. Equally, while this approach looks at large numbers, the insurance company may differentiate premiums within groups if some individuals prove to be more prone to accidents, or some sub-groups (for example young males living in rural areas) are less prone.

Estimating risk is itself difficult. One of the more common approaches to estimating it in the security context, especially when there are a number of possible factors that can cause a failure, is to use fault tree analysis; for example in the context of maritime container security, see Kumar and Verruso (2008). Developed for safety engineering and reliability engineering, it seeks to understand how systems can fail, to identify the best ways to reduce risk or at least to get a feeling for event rates of a safety accident or a particular system-level failure. While the technique is useful at showing how resistant a system is to single or multiple initiating security failures, it is not so useful at finding all possible initiating faults. An alternative approach, failure mode and effects analysis, provides a bottom-up approach to look at individual failures but cannot handle multiple failures.

Whether individuals choose to insure, or to take the risk burden themselves is also sometimes a quasi-subjective matter revolving around whether it is felt the premium for the insurance is worth the security offered. It is a question of how information is subjectively treated rather than a case of a lack of information regarding the risk per se. In other cases, and especially if the implications of the outcome affect third parties, there are often institutional requirements to have insurance, and many countries insist automobile drivers do so in order to provide some financial compensation for blameless individuals in a crash, e.g., the legal requirement of 'third-party insurance' in the United Kingdom. There are administrative costs involved in providing any form of insurance, and in some contexts large companies will insure themselves to reduce this burden.

With uncertainty it is more a matter of the judgment of those affected involving citizens' subjective probabilities. There have either been very few events in the past that allow for the use of the large numbers concept, or they have been too heterogeneous in nature to draw common pictures. In the context of public policy, in many cases, the perpetrators of events such as terrorist attacks may also be reactive to any attempt to prevent their activities in the future.

Getting a handle on, and quantifying, uncertainty is immensely difficult. One method is to make use of expert opinion asking advice from those that have some past experiences of assessing uncertainty or knowledge of the way that, for example, terrorists behave. This generally employs some sort of Delphi procedures, with the experts providing revised views in successive rounds of interviews or questionnaires as information from their fellow panel members becomes available. The idea is that this pooling of information is likely to provide a better picture of the situation or of potential counter actions than that of any individual expert. Delphi exercises can firm this up by spreading information across participants and thus enhancing the basis upon which they make their judgments.

An alternative, although it may make use of the outcome of an expert opinion assessment as a starting point, involves using Monte Carlo simulations. Such simulations build models of possible results by substituting a range of values – a probability distribution – for any factor that has inherent uncertainty.[6] The process then involves calculating results over and over, each time using a different set of random values from the probability functions. Depending upon the number of perceived uncertainties and the ranges specified for them, a Monte Carlo simulation could involve tens of thousands of recalculations before it is complete. Monte Carlo simulation produces distributions of possible outcome values that can then be treated as risk. The challenges are in defining which probability distributions to employ; this essentially is a judgment call.

What the Monte Carlo method can be helpful in is to furnish the decision-maker with a range of possible outcomes and to give guidance as to the probabilities they will occur for any choice of action. It gives insights into the extreme possibilities along with all possible consequences for middle-of-the-road decisions.

The problem of uncertainty and its implications for economic actions was clearly articulated in a more general sense by John Maynard Keynes (1937), albeit in a macroeconomic context,

> [Under uncertainty] there is no scientific basis on which to form any calculable probability whatever. We simply do not know. Nevertheless, the necessity for action and for decision compels us as practical men to do our best to overcome the awkward fact and to behave exactly as we should if we had behind us a good Benthamite calculation of a series of perspective advantages and disadvantages, each multiplied by its appropriate probability waiting to be summed.[7]

In the absence of a Gaussian probability, more subjective views and pragmatic policies therefore come into play. Holding an arbitrary 'reserve' to cover losses is one approach, but not normally practical in the private sector for potentially major adverse events because of what are essentially the high inventory holding costs involved. This is often why governments act to provide compensation after an adverse and unpredictable event such as an earthquake: 'An act of God'. It effectively acts as a sort of insurer of last resort. Terrorist attacks are infrequent and diverse in nature, as well as in their impacts making risk assessment virtually impossible; hence this governmental approach is often taken regarding security matters, and is why in many cases the government implicitly provides at least a minimum level of cover.

One of the difficulties with providing the optimal level of security is that the actions of those involved are motivated by subjective probabilities rather than by Gaussian risk, objective probabilities. This means that from a statistical perspective a terrorist event using, say, a container to carry a bomb can cause an overreaction from governments, maritime shipping firms and the general public because of the lack of a clear idea of the motivation of the perpetrators. There may also be an excessive perception of the risks from shipping container carriers in our example by those in the maritime shipping network. Further, there may be unwillingness on the part of the general public to accept an objective level of risk even if it is provided with hard data. People simply do not accept the situation, in part because of a lack of prior experience if previous events have not affected them. This is not just an issue in security but is common in other areas of human activity, for example it partly explains why younger people are less risk averse, even when cognizant of the nature of threats confronting them. It also explains a proclivity for people to overinsure.

While one can draw some useful, if not definitive, distinctions between the challenges posed by transportation safety – largely a risk situation – and those associated with transportation security – largely a matter of uncertainty – the border between the two cases is not clearly defined. In particular some types of security issue do involve large numbers of incidents of a fairly uniform kind that have resulted in quite extensive insurance markets or companies embracing the notion that they are a calculable cost of doing business. This situation is particularly so in the case of small-scale pilfering and vandalism. Car insurance, for example, in many countries often includes fire and theft, and tourists can insure themselves against theft and for medical costs should they be attacked.

There are often systematic differences regarding the types of cars that are stolen or vandalized or where the incidents occur, and when there are numerous events a fairly reliable estimate of probabilities can be obtained. If this leads to various actions to reduce incidents because of the premiums involved, this may result in perpetrators changing their behavior but this is likely to be a longer-term and observable change. On the other hand not all safety issues are easy to predict and thus actuarial calculations pose problems – the impact of very rare climatic events such as flooding or storms on the transportation network is one example, and the mechanical failure of a hitherto safe component in a commercial aircraft is another.

There are also important issues of moral hazard involved in insurance markets. These entail those who pay premiums relaxing their stance regarding self-protection. If you have insurance against theft of your vehicle, there is less reason to lock it, remove the ignition keys when parked or to put the windows up – if it is stolen then the insurance company will pay. This ultimately pushes up premiums for the entire car-owning cohort. Another way of looking at it is that unless there is some good idea of how many car owners will act in this way, and of the response of criminals to their actions, the final crime rate and premiums are uncertain, although once a quasi-equilibrium is reached, reasonably accurate actuarial calculations can be made.

There are also problems when it comes to probability of accidents and some types of security infringements. While actuarial calculations, or something approaching them, are possible they can be complex and time consuming. This means that they are largely the domains of experts and, for the system to be fully efficient, those with the potential to be adversely affected have largely to accept the experts' calculations and premiums offered for insurance cover. The evidence is that most people are often far more risk averse than they should be, and thus tend, as noted earlier, to pay for more insurance than strict, objective calculations indicate they really need. One reason for this may just be the asymmetry of information concerned – the actuarial calculations of the insurance companies are just not to be trusted.[8] Another reason is that safety concerns vary in their intensity, and individuals may be much more concerned about occasional, but severe events than the average occurrence of an event or the average amount of harm done. The latter case forms the basis for deductibles in insurance plans whereby potential smaller claims are discouraged.

3.5 NOTIONS OF OPTIMAL LEVELS OF SECURITY

Defining the theoretical, optimal level of security is relatively easy in terms of basic neoclassical economics. It is where the marginal cost of an extra unit of security is equated with the marginal benefits that are generated. As with most things, however, the devil is in the detail. First, although, the basic concepts inherent in thinking about optimal security policies are fairly standard in economics; their application is not simple. I initially spend some time looking at this.

Considering the Welfare Gains of Enhanced Security

One way of accessing the benefits of increased security, or conversely the costs of poor security, is in terms of private and social surpluses. The former are essentially the benefits that individuals enjoy beyond those they pay for and the latter the larger benefits that society may enjoy from an individual adopting security measures. The second category is essentially composed of external effects, these are returned to several times later in the book.

Following Prentice and Hickson (2007), Figure 3.1 offers a stylized picture of the implications for an individual of enhanced public security.[9] MPB is the perceived marginal private benefit of additional security by an individual, MSB is the marginal public benefit, and MSC is the marginal cost of additional security.

The MPB curve can also be seen as the amount individuals are willing to pay for particular personal levels of security. Individuals will buy security to the point where their marginal benefit equals the costs of additional security, namely Q at a price of P. Because, as we discuss in detail below, there are some forms of security not available in the market because of public good issues, and there are also various externalities[10] involved in the security market, individuals may collectively want more security than the market offers; this is reflected in the MSB curve. If we take this into account, the optimum level of security provision is Q* at a cost of P*.

Any public measure or action, be it simple reassurance that makes individuals feel safer, will, however, push the marginal benefit curve of providing private security down to, say, MPB_1, with individuals now only providing Q_1 of security. On the assumption that the change in perceived

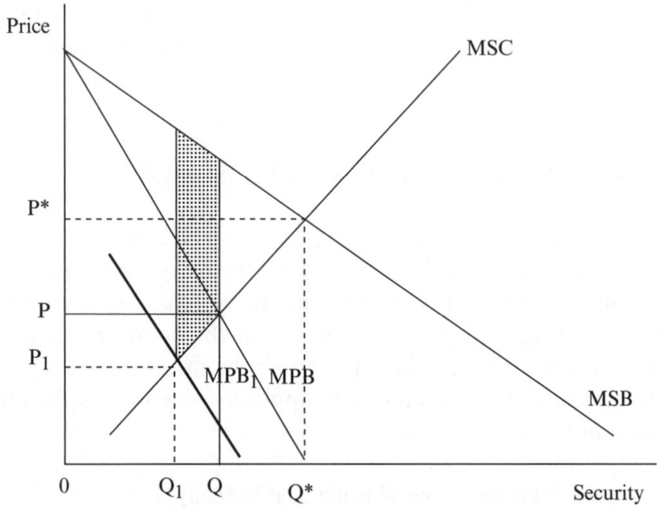

Figure 3.1 The welfare gains from a feeling of greater security

'risk', as reflected in the leftward move of the MPB, does not affect the MSB curve, and thus the social optimum is still Q*, then there is a gain seen as the shaded area. One way of interpreting this is that the government still provides and pays for QQ* of security, but individuals have more confidence in the system, and by only providing Q_1 feel that they are enjoying Q. Hence there is no cost in the provision of Q_1Q.

If, on the other hand, some terrorist event adversely affects public confidence in the existing security system, then the MSB curve will move out. People will demand more or better security from the authorities. We assume the move is to curve MSB in Figure 3.2. This will result in an increase in the combined equilibrium level of private and public security required to Q_2. The cost of this is the shaded area, which can be interpreted as the cost to government of tighter security measures.

Defining the Optimum

Figure 3.3 provides a simple abstract diagrammatic representation of the situation with security measured in some undefined way.[11] This allows an assessment of the optimal level of security that should be provided in simple cost–benefit terms under a variety of assumptions regarding such things as public perceptions and the cost efficiency of the security system. C is an upward-sloping marginal cost of security curve based on

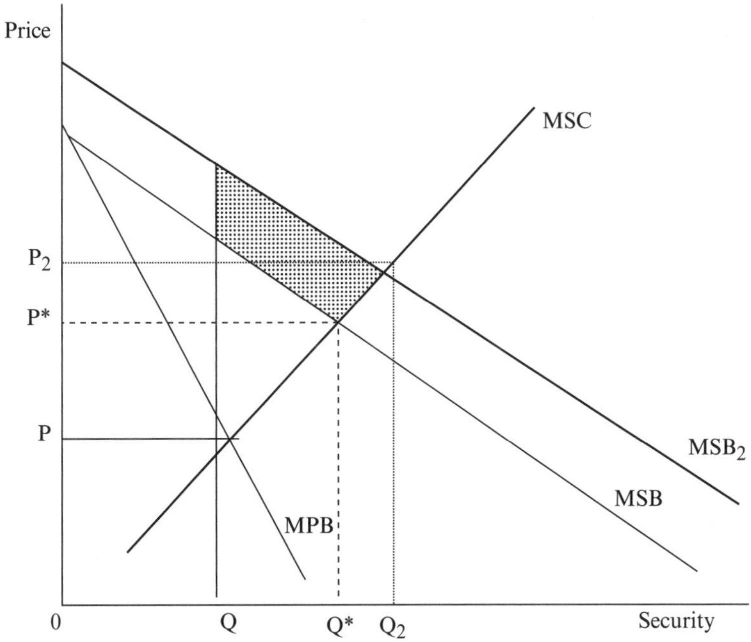

Figure 3.2 The welfare losses from a public response to increased concerns about less security

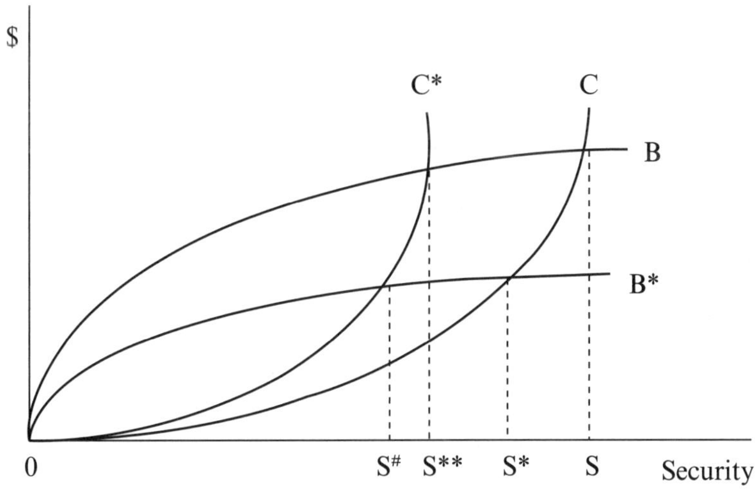

Figure 3.3 The determinants of optimal security provision

the reasonable assumption that each increment of security costs more to provide as the most basic and cheapest measures are initially adopted and subsequent ones become more sophisticated and complex. The B curve indicates the marginal benefits of additional security with the flattening of the slope reflecting the decline in additional benefits associated with the more detailed security measures. The optimal level of security in this is S.

These curves, however, can usefully be decomposed for analytical purposes. Increased security provides benefits in terms of both a reduced threat of material damage (including physical injuries to people) (separated out as B*) and greater psychological 'comfort' to those using the transportation services, living or working close to the transportation facility, or having kith or kin who are. The distance between B and B* curves represents the peace of mind that extends beyond the greater physical effects of enhanced security.[12] The extent to which this psychological 'comfort' exceeds the actual dangers that exist depends to a large extent on the information that is available to potential travelers, their perceptions, the persuasiveness of the security agency, and their degree of risk adversity.

While there may be no good estimate of the reduced chance of being involved in an attack, there are benefits from simply seeing security measures in place even if there is no objective method for assessing their effectiveness. Conversely, however, people are sensitive to such things as media coverage of threats that push out the mental benefits of greater security actions. There may also be benefits that are external to those using transportation or working in supplying it, for example to those living in the neighborhood. These externalities are side-effects of an action that positively or negatively affect a third party without any direct payments being made. Their importance in security is summed up well by Heal and Kunreuther (2005) when discussing the interdependence of systems,

> Terrorist risks are typically interdependent – the risks to which one organization, critical economic sector, or country is exposed depend not only on its own choice of security investments but also on the actions of others. Failures of any element of an interdependent system can have devastating impacts on all parts of the system.[13]

The cost curve also has its complexities.[14] Attacks can inflict both material damage on the fabric of transportation infrastructure and on vehicles, and injury and death on individuals. The C curve is drawn to separate out the minimum marginal costs of incremental units of security, including the additional inconvenience costs to all parties concerned, as well as financial outlays, but the overall economic costs may deviate from this.[15] The incentive to provide security at the lowest cost may not be there, for example because the agency involved is a monopoly or there may be principal–agent problems if it is a public undertaking or a private supplier is a monopolist. In consequence, X-inefficiency may be present in providing the security measures; for example, the efficiency of airport passenger screening has been questioned (Gkritza et al., 2006).[16] These, and other factors, can push up the cost curve. Potential inefficiency arises in these types of situation because objectives tend to be opaque and many of the costs are only indirectly borne by those responsible for the security provided.

The problem of providing security on the lowest cost curve is compounded if there is asymmetrical information concerning the effectiveness of security measures. For example, security experts and consultants have an incentive to exaggerate the challenges being faced, as have politicians; consultants are after all rent-seeking economic agents operating in a commercial market, and those seeking public support gain by appearing as protectors. In effect, there is the potential for a degree of 'regulatory capture' of the security system by those involved in providing it.

On the other hand, the costs of security measures may bring down the cost of insurance premiums by reducing other forms of crimes, such as pilferage, in the transportation supply chain. The direct costs of security measures may also be mitigated to some extent by the supply chain adjusting at other points, either up or down, as other actors modify their behavior (Gould et al., 2010). In these cases the actual cost curve will be lower than that depicted in the figure. The trade-offs involved are empirical questions and inevitably will differ according to circumstance.

Given these complexities, a number of suboptimal outcomes may emerge. For simplicity, we assume that gains at other points in the supply chain offset some of the costs of enhanced security and any X-inefficiency associated with it. In other words, $\{C^{*}-C\}$ is the difference between the full and the narrowly defined minimum financial cost curve of security.

If the attention was purely on the commercial damage that can be caused by acts of terrorism, as for example may be the case for private insurance companies, then security will be undersupplied by $\{S-S^{*}\}$. But even if the psychological benefits of more assured security are not ignored, then there may be inefficiencies in the provision of security measures due to the existence of X-inefficiency leading to inadequacies of $\{S-S^{**}\}$ in their provision if the agencies responsible do not minimize their costs. If both full benefits and costs are underestimated and the provision of security measures is not done efficiently then the resultant level of security, $S^{\#}$, could be well below the social optimum.

It is also conceptually possible, with both the costs and benefits rising and with the increased provision of security from a conceptual perspective, that the curves do not intersect because subjective risk assessment results in the perceived benefits of enhanced security measures rising faster than the costs of implementing additional security measures. As a result, the optimal outcome would be an infinite net benefit for increasing security. This is unlikely in practice because there is plenty of evidence from behavioral studies that have looked at people's choices between safe but expensive activities and cheap but more dangerous ones that risk adversity does taper off quite steeply after some point as the residual perceived danger declines.

3.6 TECHNICAL CHALLENGES IN DEFINING OPTIMAL SECURITY

While it is helpful to develop models setting out concepts such as the various forms of optima and of equilibriums that need consideration in looking at transportation security issues, they do rely on a large number of assumptions regarding the nature of security and the attitudes of individuals and groups. While many assumptions may embody a reasonable degree of underlying realism, others are more speculative, and generally quantification is difficult.

The Public Good Issue

It is sometimes useful to take an example to pinpoint some more general issues. Here we consider the numerous individual firms that handle containers as they flow through the maritime shipping network. This is both a major security challenge for most governments and an activity that highlights many of the challenges under discussion. Each individual firm's operation is interdependent with the operations of other firms. Thus, any major terrorist event will almost inevitably have severe repercussions for firms throughout the transportation network. As a result, there is very little incentive for any individual firm to enhance its security arrangements if other firms in the system have lower levels of security.

Put simply, except for the philanthropic, there is no significant advantage to one firm increasing its own security oversight because, while it may positively impact on other suppliers' security by reducing the general threat to the industry, others cannot be excluded from enjoying those benefits or be made to pay for them. In terms of competition, it actually puts the secure firm at a disadvantage; the firm pays for the additionally security but has no relative benefit in terms of competiveness. For example, the installation of an alarm system or security cameras by one warehouse provider may deter violations of other nearby warehouses if potential intruders are unaware which has the alarm or surveillance system. The 'other' warehouses can effectively free-ride on the enhanced security without bearing its costs.

In this sense, many elements of security can be seen as meeting the economists' definition of a pure public good in that it has significant elements of both non-excludability (one cannot be excluded from the benefits enjoyed by the actions of another) and non-rivalness (one's consumption of a good provided by another does not diminish the latter's consumption).[17]

In market conditions, because of the difficulty of charging for them – the 'free-rider' problem – there is a lack of financial incentive for public goods to be adequately provided. As a result they are often seen as requiring some form of external public policy to either coerce the appropriate supply from the private sector, or for the state to provide the public good itself. National defense and mass immunizations are often cited as the classic cases where this is needed and occurs.

An optimal container security policy, for example, involving both public and private risk-bearing, would mean private actions by those directly involved with the shipment of containers, with national and international authorities having a more public role. In this sense, there is essentially a need to rethink container security in terms of an interdependent network rather than the security of individual containers. Both public and private interests come into play, but teasing out the exact role of each together with their implicit respective financial contributions is difficult.

Private Incentives of Logistics Firms

We remain with the idea that insecurity of containers in the maritime shipping network potentially has both a commercial and a social cost. Commercial risk of physical danger can be insured against but at a cost, but losses associated with a loss of business are normally uninsurable, or are at least have ceilings attached. Firms in the maritime shipping network have a commercial interest in providing an acceptable, albeit not optimal, level of security for the containers that they handle. Maritime shipping firms and their customers are naturally concerned with the safety and security of their hardware and with the goods in transit. Further, they both have spent considerable energy in building up their own unique customer franchises and quality of service and need to protect their investments.

The demand for container-based services is a derived demand, derived from the producers and distributers of products. Individual firms will simply adopt the Charles Tiebout (1956) approach if there are unacceptable levels of container insecurity – they will vote with their feet and take their shipping needs to maritime shipping outlets that offer what they perceive as acceptable levels of security. Maritime shipping firms would have to retain their clients by offering more security and less profitable shipping rates. The problem is compounded because insecurity not only affects individual businesses but it can affect ports and nations.

Maritime shipping firms may be cognizant of these types of effects and act to minimize risk, but objective assessment of many elements may be blurred. The insurance market, because of its large experience, can often inject a clearer, actuarial view into the decision process. Basically, if a maritime shipping firm has insecurities in its operations then this would be reflected in their insurance costs. The problem, as with all matters of security, is that insurance is based upon previous experiences and these may be too limited to provide a reasonable estimate of the magnitude of the actuarial risk involved. Insurance companies will then themselves exercise judgment that inevitably tends towards risk aversion. Premiums would be suboptimally high even if available.

Free-rider Issues

There is an old adage that networks are only as strong as their weakest link, and that applies to transportation security; because of this there can be a tendency towards underinvestment in security, a point made by Hal Varian (2004) regarding communications. Basically, even if the optimal level of security at each stage in a supply chain can be determined, if any element in that chain is less secure than this then the incentive is for other actors to reduce their security level. Essentially, their own cost–benefit calculations will suggest it is not worth maximizing their efforts to be secure. The result is a deviation of the equilibrium level of investment, a Nash equilibrium is obtained in Varian's analysis that deviates from the socially optimal supply.

The argument also holds, as we have seen earlier, if any agent in the supply chain puts additional security into their activity; given the decreasing marginal benefits of such measures in general, this will probably result in other agents in any linked transportation system reducing their investments and free-riding on the investors' heightened security. The policy response to this may included mandatory coordination between those involved in the various links of the transportation chain, or as Adib Kanafani and Jiangchuan Huang (2010) suggest, more motivated agencies bribing the less motivated to upgrade their security. The latter, compensation-based approach is clearly second best.

Capture of Security Policy

There are financial economic rents to be derived from the supplying security services. If this were not the case there would be no private security services. There are profits to be made by offering consultancy advice, providing hardware, policing security systems and so on. This can occur when there are economies of scale in providing security services and the transportation supplying undertakings is not of sufficient size to benefit fully from these, but specialist security firms are. There may also be economies of specialization, whereby certain types of movement are so infrequent and particular that specialized security measures are needed. It is possible in these cases for private sector security providers, because of their size or expertise, to capture the market and influence security requirements.

Inevitably therefore, there is a tendency for various commercial groups to seek to capture at least some of these financial rents. Given the inevitability of political considerations getting involved in security, there is also the prospect of capture by those responsible for defining the framework of the system (basically 'pork barrel' politics). Essentially, the political process allows for rent to be sought in term of votes. This, for example, can take the form of exaggerating threat to gain public support, a strategy often used by extreme political groups to justify their taking control.

One of the problems is the difficulty of defining exactly what the economic nature of the security 'good' is. This lack of clarity often leads to the mistaken view that it is always a public good that is both non-rival and non-excludable. Given the costs of securing the transportation networks, the need to coordinate the special skills that may be required, combined with the nature of the uncertainty involved, some form of government involvement is inevitable. The challenge is to be clear on why this is so, and to assess whether the net costs of any intervention failures associated with official bureaucratic involvement are actually less than the costs of the market failures they seek to contain.

While some security measures may be undertaken directly by government agencies, there has been a trend towards outsourcing in many areas, but most notably utilities, over the past twenty years. The intent is to ensure that X-inefficiency is minimized and thus the maximum level of security can be attained from a given budget. Tendering has become commonplace as potential suppliers compete for the market (Demsetz, 1968).

The problem with this in the security context, besides a plethora of challenges with defining an appropriate auctioning system, is that of quality control. Tendering can be done in a number of ways. In many cases a clear output is specified and the supplier willing to provide this at lowest cost wins the contract. This sort of approach has been used in such domains as airport screening of passengers, in the checking of shoppers and their bags at malls, and has the potential for the screening of maritime containers. Security patrols at ports offer another possibility. The difficulties lie in two broad areas. There is the need to define an appropriate level of security service to be tendered for. This often requires rather precise descriptions that may prove inappropriate, or criteria that meet political expedience rather than strict security logic. Added to this, contracts are usually for a defined period that gives little flexibility to react to changing circumstances during the contract.

Second, there is scope for capture of the system by the private companies offering services. This can be at the initiation level of tendering as these companies lobby the political process to set security criteria close to their own 'product'. Capture can also be at the renewal phase if there are fixed costs or economies of experience that give incumbents an advantage.

International Externalities

In the simplest sense, systems, including transportation, are particularly prone to fail when those guarding them do not suffer the full costs of failure. The full costs of failure are, in microeconomic jargon, partly external to the decision-making of this 'guardian'. The problem is one that exists both within domestic transportation systems and within international networks. As an example of the latter, lax security at an airport in one country may result in a hijacking and the plane being used as a 'guided bomb' in another country; the first country has no automatic incentive to prevent this other than it may lose some future aviation business. Essentially, a security system is only as strong as its weakest link in this case. But, conversely, there are also positive externalities associated with a country tightening its security so that others need not fear it being the base for an attack, although again there is often limited incentive for doing this if the country that acts receives no additional benefits or has at least some of its expenses refunded.

Geoffrey Heal and Howard Kunreuther (2005) provide a good example of this type of situation in the context of explaning the Pan Am Flight 103 incident in 1988 (the Lockerbie bombing). The bomb was planted in Malta where there was minimal security; it then passed through both Frankfurt am Main and London Heathrow Airports, which had tighter security for baggage originating at these points, but transit bags were not inspected. The bomb, designed to explode at 28 000 feet, an altitude reached over the Atlantic, subsequently did just that.

Maritime transportation has a large international component and security poses similar issues. Security is again only as good as the weakest link in the system and this may be threatened by a lack of international incentive to prevent attacks on the logistics chain. The problem may be seen in this context: a failure of governments to agree on a mechanism for property rights allocations because of the capture of the system by their own populations. An example of this is that many states have failed to implement security agreements in the past. The underlying challenge is that there are failures in the institutional structure to handle such international issues; a problem that can be illustrated using the September 2001 attacks in the US that subsequently raised significant concerns that containers, rather than just aircrafts, may be used to carry out or facilitate terrorist attacks.

The very large number of containers, the thousands of firms and the multitude of individuals involved in container shipping, and limited government oversight over the global supply chain make confronting this concern difficult. Further, organized crime has long used containers to smuggle narcotics, weapons, people and other contraband, making it reasonable to assume that terrorist groups may utilize containers to further their own ends. Containers are, however, an integral component of a global supply chain that has been designed to be fast and efficient. As we see in Chapter 8, a terrorist attack that utilized containers and the maritime supply chain could not only damage the short- and long-term credibility of the entire global logistics system, but it could damage the psyche of a nation's citizens. Terrorism is ultimately about inflicting psychological damage. A loss of faith in the integrity of the world's maritime shipping system would represent a major terrorist victory.

The focus of this study is not on the technical apparatus available to enhance container, and other aspects of international transportation, security, but rather on the institutional and economic factors that will ultimately influence the effectiveness of security policies for the international transportation network. International trade has grown over the past decades in part due to international initiatives involving multinational and bilateral relaxation of institutional barriers to international commerce, but also as the result of important managerial and technology developments. The result has been the creation of sophisticated passenger and freight supply chains that has reduced the costs of trade in goods and opened up a variety of new markets for travelers. Recent concerns over the security of this structure are, however, beginning to increase costs in the supply chain, both directly, as new security measures are legislated, and as private suppliers are adopting their own measures for commercial reasons.

3.7 COST–BENEFIT ANALYSIS

A widely used technique in public policy assessment is cost–benefit analysis (or benefit–cost analysis as it is often called in the United States), and this has been adopted in a number of cases in an attempt to get a handle on the economic 'value' of alternative security options at various levels of aggregation, regarding alternative strategies, applying different instruments and so on.

In contrast to a narrow commercial approach, investments involving the public sector generally involve considerations based upon welfare economics and thus employ some form of cost–benefit analysis. Cost–benefit analysis is a practical way of assessing the desirability of projects and was initially developed in France during the 1840s, but refined during the 1930s by the US Corps of Engineers, where it is important to take a long view (in the sense of looking at repercussions in the further as well as the nearer future) and a wide view (in the sense of allowing for side-effects of many kinds on many persons, industries, regions and so on). That is, it implies the enumeration and evaluation in monetary terms of all the relevant costs and benefits.[18] Mathematically, it can be expressed as defining a boundary, the net present value of a project, exceeding which produces a net social benefit.

$$NPV_{SW} = \sum_{G=1}^{G=x} \sum_{t=1}^{T=K} \left(\frac{aP(B_{GT}) - bP(L_{GT})}{(1 + i)^T} \right) \tag{3.1}$$

where: NPV_{SW} is the social net present value; $aP(B_{GT})$ is the probable social benefit B to be enjoyed by individual G in year T as a result of a security measure; B_{GT} is given a weighting a, to reflect society's welfare preference for protecting members of group G; $bP(L_{GT})$ is the probable social cost L imposed on group G in year T as a result of the investment's completion. L_{GT} is given a weighting b, to reflect society's welfare preference for group G; i is the relative social weight attached to a cost or benefit occurring as the result of the security measure in a given year T; K is the anticipated duration of the measure; and x is the number of groups affected.

From the economic perspective, any action that passes as a cost–benefit assessment with a NPV_{SW} exceeding zero should increase security as defined in Equation 3.1, and if there are alternatives that pass this test, then the one with the greatest incremental net benefit is preferred.

In the US, cost–benefit analysis, or at least some variants of the technique, has been widely adopted as a criterion for the allocation of public expenditures. It is regularly applied, in some instances since 1995 in the US, by statute to assess investment project and regulatory reforms in transportation, water resource, health, education, urban development and renewal, species conservation, and safety. A variant, cost-effectiveness analysis that considers the cheapest way of meeting particular objectives is also used in these sectors and also has relevance for deciding security policies. Given the widespread use of these types of assessment tools, there is an argument for their adaptation and use when considering security issues to provide a degree of consistency across the various areas of public expenditure and control.

Cost–benefit analysis theoretically involves a comprehensive approach to both the costs and benefits of improving transportation security. There are problems in identifying many of these, as we have seen, and we will not dwell on these, but in addition there are problems in ensuring that no double counting is involved in the arithmetic. This can pose problems given the various overlapping groups that may result from improved security. For example, in a cost–benefit calculation the aim is to be comprehensive, but this poses challenges when simply adding the immediate benefits does not encapsulate the wider tangible and intangible gains not only to the individuals directly affected but to society more generally.

The benefits of improved transportation security, as Barry Prentice (Prentice and Hickson, 2007) has emphasized, are diverse even in the general case, and often multiply as the more specific the security action is. Prentice provides, using Canada as the example, a convenient classification of the main effects according to whether they are intended (the direct effects), or not (the indirect effects), and whether they can be quantified using market prices (the tangible effects), or not (the intangible effects). He further examines the four broad types of security measures set out in Table 3.2 to reflect the main parties affected, and highlights possible overlaps that can occur in estimating the impacts of security measures.

Sovereignty protection in the context of transportation involves the security of foreign business, travel and financial transactions. It is aimed at facilitating seamless trade and international mobility with benefits to the companies and citizens of the countries involved. It not only involves physical protection from attack but also smuggling and the 'invasion' of alien flora and fauna. The increased interoperability of hardware and software that it affords allows greater economic efficiency and fosters more trade, leading to enhanced economic performance.

At the meso-level, terrorism prevention, in addition to limiting the immediate economic damage that terrorist acts can inflict on the supply chain, generally reduces the costs of insurance, and increases the demand for economic activity such as tourism. There may also be indirect benefits if the prevention policies lead to a greater standardization of equipment and protocols across countries that extend out from security to other aspects of doing business, such as safety and financial practices. There are also micro psychological benefits if individuals feel safer.

Interdiction of illegal activities takes advantage of the many synergies that exist between terrorism and civil crime prevention, with their exploitation leading to fewer personal crimes. Such linking means that crimes become more difficult to perpetrate and with this reduction in

Table 3.2 The tangible and intangible benefits of transportation security

	Direct benefits	Indirect benefits
Sovereignty protection		
• Tangible benefits	Compliance with Canadian regulations	Interoperability of the supply chain
	Reduction of smuggling and illegal activities	Expansion of trade
	Control of foreign disease and pests	
• Intangible benefits	Enhanced sovereignty	Culture of law obedience
	Fair immigration practice	
	Protection of flora and fauna	
Terrorism prevention		
• Tangible benefits	Reduced risk premiums	Lower supply chain costs
	Maintenance of tourism	Development of security technology
	Higher property values	
• Intangible benefits	Open border for US trade	Travelers feel safer
	Better inter-jurisdictional coordination	
Interdiction of illegal activities		
• Tangible benefits	Reduced risk premiums	Lower supply chain costs
	Lower staff costs	
	Crime does not pay so well	
• Intangible benefits	Better inter-jurisdictional coordination	Reduced managerial stress
		Travelers feel safer
		Culture of law obedience
Personal security		
• Tangible benefits	Reduced risk premiums	Higher asset values
	Employment losses, medical expenses, etc.	
	Computer security	
• Intangible benefits	Improved crime prevention	Transfer of fear to real risk
	Reduced stress and inter-group tension	

Source: Adapted from Prentice and Hickson (2007).

actuarial risk, insurance premiums decrease, stimulating business as well as leaving individuals with more disposable income. In the case of businesses that self-insure, it reduces the level of 'policing' costs involved, although, as we see later, it may simply push the costs onto other vulnerable groups.

At the micro level, personal security, as with the wider considerations, also can reduce insurance costs, and with this may come additional indirect benefits of higher asset values, especially if there are positive community effects. There is also potentially less social stress as individuals feel more secure about those that they interact with. But there are moral dangers if the insured become 'reckless' and fail to act responsibly.

NOTES

1. This is a particular point emphasized by the Public Choice School of economics.
2. Kanafani and Huang (2010) summarize the situation well: 'The little we know about transportation security suggests increased vulnerability at points of inter-modal connection or at large scale termini, where two conditions arise: large numbers of people making transfers and an institutional ambiguity regarding who is responsible for securing the system. This ambiguity can result in unbalanced and inefficient security investment. For example while large amounts of money are spent on securing an airport, little or nothing, is done to secure the shuttle buses that penetrate deep into the airport infrastructure!'
3. For a discussion of the role of air transportation in international trade, see Button and Pels (2010).
4. Although in the case of determining the actual physical nature of an incident, whether it is an accident or a deliberate malicious act, countries often have a single agency (such as the US National Transportation Safety Board). Subsequent analysis, once the cause of the event is known, may then, when relevant, be passed to security authorities; in the US context this happens if the Attorney General declares the case to be linked to an intentional criminal act.
5. This seems to have been ignored in many policy statements. For example, regarding the UN's International Maritime Organization (2002a) International Ship and Port Facility Security Code, we find, '. . . the Code takes the approach that ensuring the security of ships and port facilities is basically a risk management activity' and that to determine what security measures are appropriate, 'An assessment of the risks must be made in each particular case to determine what security measures are appropriate.' The purpose of the Code is to provide a standardized, consistent framework for evaluating risk, enabling governments to offset changes in threat with changes in vulnerability for ships and port facilities. How the 'risk' of terrorist attacks is to be estimated is not stated.
6. The RAND Corporation's study of TSA actions provides a good example of a major Monte Carlo exercise involving transportation security (Morral et al., 2012).
7. From an economic policy perspective, one way of looking at this is to develop the ideas of Frank Ramsey (1931), who argued that by observing people's reactions one can glean from them subjective probabilities about societies' views. This may then lay the foundation for ways of developing efficient policy responses to terrorism.
8. This goes back to the well-established problem of 'lemons' (Akerlof, 1970). There is a tendency for buyers to mistrust sellers regarding the quality of any product because they

have less information about it. In consequence they will be willing to pay less for it, or in our case take out more insurance than is optimal.

9. This approach is examined in more detail in Prentice and Hickson (2007). A similar, but simpler diagrammatic analysis is found in Coughlin et al. (2002).
10. An externality is a cost or benefit that results from an activity or transaction and which affects an otherwise uninvolved party who did not choose to incur that cost or benefit. It may either be, as here, technological, in which case it affects the total resources involved in an action, or pecuniary, in which case it leaves the resource base unaffected but involves transfers of costs and benefits.
11. Prentice (Prentice and Hickson, 2007) provides an alternative diagrammatic approach. The outcomes are largely the same, although here we derive alternative optima rather than an optimum based on the welfare of society generally. Essentially, in terms of Figure 3.1, Prentice considers various changes in the incidence of a security threat rather than differing perceptions and does not make any allowance for potential inefficiencies in provision of security services.
12. The B* curve can be seen as reflecting what is sometimes called 'citizen's subjective probabilities'. The B curve in this context shows the 'best-information subjective probabilities' based upon the opinions of experts. Alan Garner (2002), for example, provides an assessment of consumer confidence after the attacks of 2001 in the US.
13. They specifically show that an airline is less likely to invest in security as more firms in the industry fail to invest, although under reasonable assumptions the industry and the individual airline would benefit if it did invest. The rationale is that it is the insurer who is responsible for the damage done to an airline, irrespective of who causes it. If airline A had to pay or compensate for damage it causes to airline B, the insurer would have to incur greater losses after an incident. This would give it an incentive to reduce premiums for carriers causing fewer incidents. Without such an incentive, if all other carriers underinsure, then airline A has no real incentive but to do likewise.
14. This is a point made clear by Stewart and Mueller (2014) when considering if airports can be made too secure.
15. While the B and C curves are drawn as smooth functions, in practice there may well be kinks if, for example, shoppers have threshold tolerance levels to the degrees of intrusion that security will impose on them.
16. X-inefficiency is normally defined as producing a good or service at costs that exceed the minimum possible. It is associated with a lack of incentive for suppliers to be as efficient as possible; see Leibenstein (1979).
17. The term and definition goes back to Paul Samuelson (1954). There are those that argue there are few, if any, public good aspects to security, for example Hans-Herrmann Hoppe (1989). It may also be argued that when the state provides 'public goods' the provision is often excessive because it involves taking resources from the private sector where they are more highly valued.
18. A very dated, but still excellent basic account of cost–benefit analysis and the underlying assumptions needed to operationalize it are to be found in Alan Prest and Ralph Turvey (1965).

4. Links between market structure and security

Shop for security over happiness and we buy it at that price
Richard Bach

4.1 INTRODUCTION

Adopting the neoclassical microeconomic reasoning that underlies the thinking of people like Gary Becker, security can be seen as a service that can be bought and sold like most other goods or services. It may also be considered from a slightly different economic perspective, following the broad ideas of Kelvin Lancaster (1966), as an attribute of a good or service, whereby individuals treat a service as bundles of attributes, selecting services to consume according to the bundles that maximize their relative utilities including the security that they bring.

But from either perspective, there is a cost attached to providing security, as well as benefits from its purchase, and thus people can bargain with suppliers over the nature, the amount and the cost of the security to be provided. Put simply, the shotgun guard on the stagecoach in the old west was a clear cost to the traveler, but as a deterrent to a hold-up it provided a benefit. In turn, the guard's pay reflected the minimum net benefit to the stagecoach company of employing him or her, with this, in turn, being a reflection of the travelers' willingness-to-pay for protection.

In this sense, security is an input into the value chain just like any other input, and the users of security services, as with any other input, want to ensure that they get value for their money; why buy it otherwise? Equally, those supplying transportation security need to make a reasonable return for their services and for making available the hardware and software that they provide. Price acts as an important arbitrator to equate these two sides of the equation. This is equally true at the macro level as it is at the level of the individual industry or firm. Nations, albeit often implicitly, weigh up the costs and benefits of their national security policies, seeking out those that offer the greatest societal net gain.

The difficulty is that, as we have seen hinted at in Chapter 3, these sorts of sales and purchases of security can be rather more complicated than the basic economic textbook examples of markets for 'widgets' imply, or indeed than the person riding shotgun in our stage coach example would suggest. As so often in practice, the devil is in the detail.

Markets can only function efficiently when there are viable institutional arrangements allowing, and guaranteeing, the allocation of tradable property rights that provide the basis for efficient transactions to take place. This is a point the Economics Nobel Prize winner Ronald Coase (1992) forces home in the context of the decline of the Soviet Union, 'These ex-communist countries are advised to move to a market economy, and their leaders wish to do so, but without the appropriate institutions no market economy of any significance is possible.'

The quasi-public good nature of many security goods and services, however, coupled with characteristics like externalities and incomplete information, while needing to be handled, also make defining relevant institutions difficult. Governments also take into account the incidence of market outcomes regarding who gain and who lose in terms of their security, and who pays for security-enhancing policies. Thus, as we have seen in prior chapters, there have traditionally been significant government interventions in the provision and allocation of security goods and services, some directly and others in the form of institutional interventions in market processes. We look at some of the tools used to deal with these market 'imperfections' in the following chapter, while here, although there is some inevitable blurring, we pay attention more specifically to how transportation markets in themselves handle some aspects of security matters.

Within this framework, security has largely, until recent times, been treated as a policing and judicial matter, with many public good, or at least quasi-public good, features.[1] The latter are seen as stemming from the fact that protecting one person from attack, say on a train, does not stop another being at least partly protected, nor does it reduce by any large amount the protection the individual receives.[2] In many cases this protection has historically been provided by the private sector with the costs averaged across the goods or people using transportation – as with the shotgun guard on the stagecoach. If individuals want more personal protection, or greater security for any goods being moved, they can carry a weapon, such as the swordsticks favored by gentry when walking in eighteenth-century European cities, hire personal bodyguards, be accompanied by a less than friendly canine companion, or have their processions moved in a strongbox. Or they may insure themselves or possessions to pass on the risk to a third party.

The state's role in these contexts is largely to ensure that contracts between transportation suppliers and the person undertaking the travel or shipping the goods are being met, hence the existence of civil law. In addition, if there are substantial economies of scale in providing transportation unlikely to be achieved by any one company, or when there are manifest public goods issues whereby contracts cannot be completed, the authorities may act to supply security, either directly or by providing subsidies to private companies to do so. If they feel they are more efficient, the authorities may, as we have seen, also act as a sort of insurer of last resort to provide compensation when security is breached, an example being the compensation given to US airlines after airspace was closed immediately following the events of 11 September 2001. In detail, the Air Transportation Safety and System Stabilization Act (ATSSSA) provided $5 billion in immediate payments to airlines as compensation for losses resulting from the ground stop order during the four days after the attack, and for losses that the airlines were expected to incur as a result of reduced air traffic from 23 September through to the 31 December. The Act also created the Air Transportation Stabilization Board and authorized it to issue federal credit instruments, including direct loans and loan guarantees of up to $10 billion, to assist carriers whose financial survival was put at risk by the terrorist attacks and the subsequent collapse in air traffic.

The extent and nature of this type of government involvement has varied over time and with context, as has its efficiency in meeting objectives. This is not surprising given that it is inevitably reactive to largely unpredictable events.

There are also normative considerations to be weighed into the calculations. Poorer sections of society often cannot afford reasonable levels of protection. In these cases the 'State', at an appropriate administrative level, may step in and use public monies or enact regulations to ensure a minimum level of security for all citizens irrespective of their income. In the transportation context, policing the streets to prevent attacks on pedestrians or vehicles is an obvious example.

The events of 11 September 2001 in the US did not destroy this broad picture of a partial market solution for security, with government being involved when market conditions were thought to have failed, but it did bring a new focus to security matters in the country, and elsewhere. While many other countries had previously been the subject of foreign terrorist attacks and had response mechanisms in place, the US had largely been insulated from such activities on its homeland. The 1993 World Trade Center bombing and the Oklahoma City bombing of 1995 may possibly be seen as exceptions, although their scale and geographical coverage was smaller, and did not instill the broader fears of the events of 2001.[3]

One of the outcomes of the events of 11 September was a significant tightening of all transportation security regimes throughout the world, not only because of direct threats, but also because the US became increasingly concerned about the possible impacts of trends in globalization and technological interconnectivity on its internal security, a situation exacerbated when countries such as Spain and the UK were subsequently subjected to major outrages. There has been a considerable focus on the part of the US on pushing out security borders. With this has come a general movement towards more direct provision of security, or at least its use of greater command-and-control regulation, and a movement away from the more market-oriented framework.

Air transportation and the movements of individuals initially dominated much of the public debate, as did the early apportionment of large-scale security expenditure after 11 September. This was largely due to the visibility of these types of activity, and a perceived political need to provide a transparent and rapid reaction to the threat of attack to reassure the general public. Put simply, people became nervous about flying and there was a need for quick and clearly visible reassurance. There was little, if any, analysis of whether the strategy as a whole, or individual elements of it, made economic sense in a conventional way other than to think of a larger security presence becoming a pronounced attribute of air travel.

In the case of air transportation, there was also the immediate proximity of the industry to the events of 11 September that made the potential for the use of commercial aircraft as weapons very obvious. The US and other countries initially acted unilaterally, or with a degree of bilateral cooperation, to enhance their security regimes. At the same time, the International Civil Aviation Organization (ICAO), the United Nations' airline oversight body, already had in place a framework based on experiences of other types of hijacking upon which it could develop an international institutional oversight strategy. As a result, subsequent progress in putting multilateral measures in place was relatively rapid, with it often involving adjusting, extending and more thoroughly enforcing existing agreements.

With the subsequent setting up of agencies such as the Transportation Security Administration (TSA) in the US, and similar institutional developments elsewhere, there then began initiatives to shift some of the emphasis away from air transportation and the screening of individual movements, and towards such things as freight transportation and public transit. The question of the economic efficiency of alternative approaches also began to arise as national and local governments started to appreciate the financial costs of enhanced security, and as individuals and industry started reflecting on the inconvenience imposed by most security measures.

Regarding the extension of concern to other transportation modes, the container in particular began to be seen both as a means of transporting what had by then become known as 'weapons of mass destruction' into countries, and as a vehicle for placing them in positions for final delivery. But set against this, containers are vital in the continued growth in many economic activities, both nationally and internationally, and concern about threats to impede their role in delivering secure transportation services for both economic and strategic purposes could have major implications for trade and economic growth. The cost–benefit mindset in this context immediately tends towards a discussion concerning the ways that security decisions are made, and the implicit weights used in setting the wide-ranging benefits of a more secure freight supply chain against the equally diverse costs.

The political-economy question then becomes that of deciding the precise role of government in this. No government has the resources to guarantee the security of every transportation movement within its territory, or involving its international trade, especially as the depth and scope of the perceived security needs to be continually adapted and updated. This is not only a matter of financial resources, but extends down to the particular needs at the micro level of consignments and trips (Flynn, 2004).

There is thus, in practice, an inevitable mix of private and public supply of security, and the challenge is often to decide where the boundaries should most effectively be drawn, and the types of roles that the various parties should play.[4] An efficient outcome involves a clearly defined split of responsibility between the public and private sectors, or some form of public–private partnership involving joint decision-making and actions. Even formulating this broad strategy is far from simple.

This chapter looks at the types of transportation markets that exist and considers the extent to which they are likely to fail, in a general sense, in providing optimal levels of security; some specifics by industry are looked at later. Chapter 5 provides a counterbalance to this market aspect by focusing on the types of situation for which considerable regulation may be needed and the forms it can take. This is not to say, as we emphasized earlier, that markets are free from government interference; there is always an institutional context, but rather we consider the ways markets, broadly defined and more narrowly, handle security and why they may need more or less government direction.

The proposal is not to go into the specific details of an ideal transportation security market, nor to critique in any depth the security measures that have been initiated in the US or elsewhere, but rather to consider the potential links between the market structures in which transportation is supplied and the natural proclivity for suppliers to provide appropriate, in a social welfare sense, security. Without understanding how any market-based system functions, it is difficult for governments to intervene to achieve a particular objective, in this case the objective of enhanced security, if not optimal security. The focus is also exclusively on potential terrorist threats and largely ignores more traditional matters of such things as theft or hostage taking. This distinction is important because the immediate aim of terrorism is essentially destruction, either of physical property or of social cohesion, to intimidate the population, whereas the others are usually acts in which damage is purely a collateral by-product.

4.2 MARKETS IN CONTEXT

Modern economies are complex, with goods and services often involving production entailing large amounts of capital and labor, and embracing numerous interactions among the actors involved. Globalization and internationalization have added to the integrated nature of systems, and with this has come more complex networks and a greater role for transportation; our understanding of how network-based industries actually function, however, is still relatively basic.[5] More broadly, institutionally these developments, with their complex supply chains and cross-border flows, have also added to the problems of industrial policy formulation at the domestic level, and the coordination of industrial policies at the international level.

It has always been important when initiating or modifying any industrial policy to have a thorough understanding of how the target industry functions as well as the motivations of those involved in it. This applies as much to security policy as it does to anti-trust or mergers policy; for example in the latter case there has been a palpable lag in adjusting the governance structure with regard to the service sector and network industries. The difficulty is that as industry has evolved, so the internal structure and organization of business have often become more complex. This has not been helped in the transportation context by the increasing complexities of financial markets and the internationalization of sourcing, production and marketing that heavily influences it. Teasing out exactly what the underlying industrial structure is, therefore, has become more difficult, and with it the identification of vulnerable points and appropriate security measures in the chain.

But it is not just for assessing the need for direct security interventions that it is important to appreciate market structures. At the same time as industries have become international, it has become more costly for the authorities to regulate them. In the case of shipping security, for example, the sheer size of the sector, the number of containers and tons of bulk moved, the technology deployed and the geographical scope of transactions make it prohibitively costly for any country, even one as wealthy as the US, to focus purely on direct government actions. Industrial involvement and a degree of self-regulation, generally with some government oversight, are almost inevitable outcomes. Such public involvement is thus not always simply a matter of stimulating desired reactions to command-and-control instruments imposed by the law, but can also take the form of commercial incentives to develop internal security strategies and coordinated security programs with the authorities; in other words, essentially establishing formal and informal partnerships.

Added to this, a case can be made that the private sector is generally closer to its business than the public regulator or legislators. A transportation supplier knows its customers, its own suppliers and its labor force and is likely, therefore, to be more cognizant of the security threats that confront it. In this context, the role of government may be seen as making more transparent to the private entity the extent to which, and the ways in which, it can, from a wider, social perspective, handle such threats.

A major problem in putting more focus on the role of the private sector when there are security issues is that uncertainty is, as we have seen, accompanied by the absence of complete insurance markets. When the problem is one of safety, there is scope to offload risk, or to self-insure in most cases. With safety, the situation is generally fairly clear cut. Insurance companies will normally, in highly fragmented markets, bear the actuarial burden and any transaction costs of dispersing liability costs, and, in cases where the market is more concentrated and involving large firms, a higher rate of self-insurance will occur. In the latter case, companies minimize transaction costs by internalization in the standard Coasian fashion. Since, by definition, there is no outside market to distribute the costs of uncertainty, the situation is different, with many elements of it involving quasi-public goods and externalities making complete contract formulation impossible. Optimization in this case thus requires some forms of government involvement, although what this may be is often not clear.

To help security measures to be acceptable and useful, it is therefore helpful for the authorities to understand the workings of the relevant markets. It has long been appreciated, for example, that availability of information and the ability to use it affects the formation of firms and industrial structure (Coase, 1937). In the presence of some types of market structures, the inherent information that influences decisions is embedded in a limited number of firms, while in others it is dispersed across many undertakings. In the former case, the nature of optimal interventions for security reasons may be better achieved through close cooperation with businesses that have immediate access to knowledge about cost and production implications of security. In the latter, a more independent, central approach may be more logical because of the essentially reactive nature of companies operating in this form of market; none have the individual power to affect market outcomes. In these diffuse markets there is also a role for government as a consolidating agent collecting dispersed flows of information and then disseminating it across the market.

4.3 MARKETS WITHIN LARGER INSTITUTIONAL FRAMEWORKS

There has been something of an intellectual transformation in the way that many economists now view markets. The 'New Institutional Economics' importantly sets the neoclassical economics of the nineteenth century that underlies most of the more traditional work on market structures, including that in the maritime field, in a larger context (Button, 2005).[6]

Figure 4.1 is a borrowed and simplified diagram from a survey paper by Oliver Williamson (2000) that sets out four levels of social analysis that can be used to put neoclassical analysis and its near relations in a more analytically complete framework. It is fairly self-explanatory: the dark arrows show constraints that come down from higher levels of analysis, while the dashed arrows show the direction of potential feedback. The information in parentheses is meant to be a crude guideline to the frequency in years over which change takes place; there is no firm pattern and so these should be treated as just indicative.

One immediate implication that emerges from the figure is that markets are more likely to react rapidly to any disruption, say by a terrorist attack, than will lawmakers who are responsible for the implementation of the legal system, that is, for governance. This is not, however, necessarily a negative thing if those implementing the laws play a sort of buffer role in adjusting their approach to existing rules and regulations, thereby smoothing out transition and limiting any stranded cost effects. Sudden, often knee-jerk changes in the market can be wasteful if they make certain technologies and human skills redundant too rapidly when the longer-term implications of an attack are unclear.

A cursory read of the literature on transportation economics, both the published and gray, quickly reveals a dominance of focus on prices, output and incentive structures, the uppermost box in the figure. This reflects typical neoclassical economic questions that form the basis of Alfred Marshall's (1890) *Principles* and underlie work on market structures. Although this type of work has become technically more advanced, and far more quantitative in its orientation over the years, its current focus and ethos would certainly not be out of place in the learned journals of the

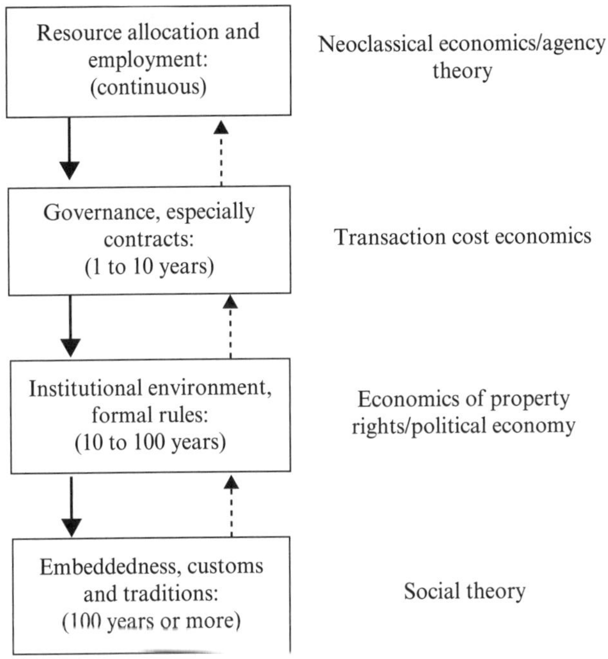

Source: Developed from Williamson (2000).

Figure 4.1 Characterization of where institutions become important

late nineteenth century. But there is also an emergent body of economics literature on transportation that is beginning to fill some of the other levels of analysis relevant to Figure 4.1, and this may prove to be of more enduring interest as well as having implications for the way security is looked at and as public policies evolve.

Longer-term issues tend to receive more attention the further one moves down the figure from narrow resource allocation matters towards transaction cost economics, the second box in the figure. Governance is important, and here the emphasis is on Coasian notions of contracts. In, say, the aviation case, this may be seen as modifying airport security measures as new technologies come online without any need to change laws. Staying with aviation, there are also contractual issues involved within the larger integrated supply chain, that, for example, tie airlines to other elements in the system such as airports and air traffic control. This may involve interpretation by the authorities of such things as the responsibility for the secure transfer of bags from one airline to another at an airport. This intellectually raises questions about how an industry should be defined in terms of governance (air transportation as one entity or airlines/airports/air traffic control as separate industries), but from a security perspective it has importance in minimizing gaps through which potential threats may penetrate. The security arrangements for any airline should, for example, fit with those for airports.

The institutional (third) box refers to longer-term changes in largely legal arrangements. These may be viewed as such things as the development of national and international legal institutional structures designed to deal with security matters. The formation of the TSA in the United States is a classic case of a change in institutions. Government importantly includes the issue of property rights and their enforcement. Traditional Pigouvian externalities (Pigou, 1920) have been areas of interest, with matters of property rights regarding pollution and safety being heavily researched areas by economists, but with security now coming more to the fore, although the academic literature on this is still embryonic. How these legal structures emerge and evolve is often complex, tied inexplicably with the political priorities of the time, and can often be highly discrete and reactive, as illustrated by the security legislation passed in the US immediately following the events of 2001. Inertia, coupled with infrequent crisis management, is a common feature.

Finally, there are the very long-term social and cultural characteristics that become embedded in markets and institutions (the fourth box). In the transportation context, we may perhaps treat the gradual move to globalization and the structural changes that go with it as such a factor. Consideration of this level of institutional development is beyond our scope other than that, in the very long term, it does inevitably involve geopolitical matters that ultimately determine the level of international terrorist activity in the world.

The relevance of looking at market structures in the stylized, institutionally based framework seen in Figure 4.1 is that, in the very short term it helps show what determines the reaction of companies to the new security-conscious environment, for example, the rates that are set and the markets that are chosen to be served, given a changed demand situation. In the longer term, companies may adjust their business models and the ways in which they interact in existing markets. In the particular context of security, for example, with potentially high capital costs being associated with many of the changes in governance being initiated and network overlaps, collusive actions may take different forms as time passes and lessons are learned. After a period, there will be formal institutional measures requiring legal compliance; reaction, however, will also be influenced again by the way in which the authorities perceive the relevant markets to work.

This type of analysis does break down to some extent when there are major external shocks to the economic system that are seen to be more than transient. The particular concern with security and terrorism that emerged after the events of 11 September 2001 would seem to fall into this category. The deviation, however, is less extreme than superficial analysis may indicate. The markets did adjust. Insurance companies, for example, began to specifically treat terrorist acts as outside the normal market and many market players, without any explicit government actions to force them to do so, did incur additional costs to reduce vulnerability and increase resilience.

The major effect, in terms of Figure 4.1, was that there were relatively immediate institutional changes, although others were rather slower to materialize as information and options shifted, and equipment became available. Normally, major institutional changes take up to a century to evolve, but, in particular, because of the effectiveness of the terrorist attacks in damaging the morale of United States citizens, the changes were more revolutionary in nature than many other reforms have been. Overall, however, the framework seen in the figure emerges as remarkably robust.

4.4 SOME MARKET STRUCTURES OF INTEREST[7]

The numerous forms of market structure found in transportation are influenced by the physical nature of the goods and people being moved, the types of consumers involved, the nature of the technology used, and the institutional set-up in which the system functions. These factors also influence the way that security is handled, and raise questions about the degree to which government involvement is needed under different market structures, and the form that this may best take.

Our understanding of many transportation markets is actually quite good after many years of study, often in the context of regulatory design or litigation, but for some markets it is less so. The exact market form for the container shipping industry, for example, is actually relatively poorly understood despite its importance in world trade and the challenges it has faced from the late 1990s in terms of piracy. There is no consensus on the underlying market structure, and a number of quite conflicting views exist. This may be in part because no single market structure exists due to variations in local conditions, differences in technology, or to continual dynamic forces being at work. Essentially no generic model fits all circumstances. The same is true of some other transportation markets, especially when they do not function in a static world or are the subject of rapid technological changes.

This would imply that while there may be circumstances where a largely uniform, generic approach to security may be appropriate, there are cases where a more bespoke approach to security policy is needed. Nevertheless, market structures do seem to matter in practice, and also do matter in the eyes of some policy-makers involved in security. We consider some of the more important market structures, and consider how transportation industries tend to fit within them, and the potential implications this has for their internalization of security threats.

Although generalizing about these things is difficult, we can say a few words about the nature of the 'security challenge' for transportation under different market structures.

Contestable and Competitive Markets

The idea that potential, as well as actual, competition can be a potent force in tempering the actions of incumbent firms goes back to the nineteenth century. Its more recent manifestation has been in the form of contestable market theory developed in particular by William Baumol et al. (1982) over a quarter of a century ago. Within the broader framework of contestability lies the more traditional idea of competitive markets where there is actual competition between existing suppliers.

From a security perspective, a market that is easy to enter and exit can pose major problems. The highly contestable nature of such a market provides little surplus revenue and, at the margin, no surplus revenue for transportation companies or incentive to finance any form of security structure beyond the minimum stipulated by regulators. In a pure contestable market, the competition within the market, or for the market, forces pricing down to the level where marginal costs are recovered but no more. This has important ramifications for the long-term stability of any industry where there are fixed costs; it becomes impossible for these costs to be recovered and this lack of an economic core leads to instability and, ultimately, to undersupply. These are hardly conditions conducive to self-administered security regimes.

The intensity of the contestable environment has the further implication that there is no mechanism for any form of agreement or contract between the companies to develop common security initiatives. Such initiatives are inevitably costly and, with free entry and exit, there is nothing to prevent new entry at lower costs and without adopting the common security measures. In a way, the entrants become free-riders in a market seen by outsiders as secure unless the entrants are identifiable. The uniform nature of the underlying services supplied means that any group seeking to provide a public service by differentiating itself by introducing additional security measures will not attract business; the customer reacts to private services attributes, not to any public externality benefits.

If the market is, therefore, genuinely contestable, or even imperfectly so, there is little by way of self-motivation to initiate security measures. The role of the international and national authorities inevitably becomes one of imposing, monitoring and policing command-and-control measures.

The advantage of such measures, from an institutional perspective, is that the largest burden of cost is immediately placed on the transportation industry; there is a need for supplying companies to conform to standards and to use prescribed technologies. For example, the imposition by the US of its 'implement-and-amend' regulatory approach (US Government Accountability Office, 2004) placed the burden of maritime security squarely on the shoulders of the shipping lines. And, in this case, the fragmented nature of the industry limited its 'voice' to articulate the implications of these costs and put forward alternative approaches. A major problem however in a transportation industry like shipping that deploys a variety of technologies and vintages of capital, is that, while easier to monitor and enforce, 'one-standard-fits-all' policies can harm economic efficiency at the margin, and leave stranded costs in the short term.

Oligopolies

The large size of many transportation companies leads to them being viewed as actors in oligopolistic markets with the scale of each giving it a degree of market power. Traditionally, market power is seen as being enhanced by such service features as the offering of integrated transportation services (for example, global courier delivery companies such as FedEx) and by various measures to capture customers (such as frequent flyer loyalty programs in the context of large airlines). The main interest of academics in oligopolies has traditionally been in the nature of the competition between suppliers, and how they seek to maximize their profits or other objectives – in particular the relationships that exist between their long- and short-term market perceptions.

From a security perspective, the way that firms operate in an oligopolistic industry, and the mechanisms by which they seek to gain market power may well be influenced by the ways in which terrorist externalities are treated. While it is not possible, by definition, to say that any company is actually more secure from terrorism than any other company (the calculus is not available), it is possible for companies to market 'security' in the same way that any other beneficial attribute can be marketed (for example, purveyors of 'miracle patent cures' have done very well in the medical field in the past). Since terrorists seek primarily to inject fear into a population, with actual physical damage being simply an input into this process, confidence in a service adds both to its social value, and to the price at which it can be sold. Just as terrorism is a psychological weapon, so the perception of a secure system is at least a partial treatment of any threat and can be marketed as such.

The cost of providing these 'security' features involves making trade-offs against the additional revenues that can be gained. The market power enjoyed by a transportation company in an oligopolistic market provides the opportunity to raise revenues to cover these costs, although the nature of the internal business game determines whether it actually materializes. The interest of the public authorities in these circumstances is to give a stamp of approval to these features so that public confidence is enhanced, and the psychological damage done by terrorism is minimized. In a way this can be viewed as a form of public–private partnership, a structure we discuss later. It implies a fairly close measure of interaction and coordination between individual transportation companies and national security authorities. This can apply not only to a single component of any supply chain, but also to an entire chain or several components of it.

Cartels

The conventional view is that any cartel, and these include such things as alliances in the international maritime sector and airlines, involves collusion with the objective of exploiting market power, even if this may be quite limited. Cartels may use this power for a variety of reasons: to maximize profit; to ensure a steady revenue flow; to recover fixed costs; to exploit economies of scale, density and scope; to generate economies of market presence, and so on. The economic impact of a cartel and, *ipso facto*, its implications for security, however, generally depends on its exact nature and the nuances of the way in which it functions.

The traditional idea of cartels is that they are formed to maximize the profits from the monopoly power created. This need not, however, lead to traditional problems of Harberger welfare losses in situations where extensive fare or rate discrimination is practiced by cartel members – a common practice found in airline and shipping cartels. The rate discrimination in itself does not, therefore, affect efficiency but only the distribution of economic rents; the air alliance companies gain and the passengers and consignees lose, but joint economic gains are maximized. Others, however, have pointed to the X-inefficiency that exists in transportation cartels; they have less incentive to minimize costs. In the absence of rate competition they can also provide an excessive quality of service or of capacity, often called 'gold-plating'. Profit maximizing may also not be the organization's objective, or at least the objective of its management. There are long-standing arguments, for example, that shipping liners seek to collude with the intent of sales-revenue maximization (Heaver, 1973).

From a security perspective it is, therefore, important to understand how a cartel is structured and operates. For example, if the collusion leads to rent capture by the cartel, this provides a reservoir of resources that can be 'taxed' by the members for security measures either by fiscal transfers or by security regulations imposed internally within the cartel. If, on the other hand, cartels exist primarily in the context of a highly competitive market to allow members to cover their fixed costs, and no economic rent is generated, then the scope for internal funding of security actions is akin to that of a contestable market. This situation occurs when there is a so-called 'empty core'.

But even in the latter case, cartels can provide the security authorities with an institutional structure to which they can devolve some of the responsibilities for developing and enforcing security measures. This potentially goes beyond the benefits that may accrue from the existence of a non-cooperative oligopolistic market. Cartels are organizational bodies with a tradition not only of ensuring the effective internal operations of the cartel and dealing with internal conflicts, but also of acting as the external voices and negotiators of the collectivity of the suppliers. This provides a single point of contact between an industry and national agencies, with the former acting as a coordinator, communicator and enforcer from the intra-industry perspective. Cartels thus have the potential to pressure their individual members into following a security driven agenda that meets larger, group objectives, and those of public authorities.

4.5 THE SECURITY 'INDUSTRIES'

The focus so far has been almost entirely on market forces and transportation industries that are directly confronted with security threats, and thus for which security is one of their costs of production. But there are also a number of private sector industries that provide various forms of security services and contribute to the supply side of the security market.[8]

These undertakings range from companies that offer protective services that reduce the probability of an attack of some kind, that provide training to those working in the transportation sector, to those that guarantee remittances to compensate for damage done to individuals and property attacked. In some cases there are combined services that, for example, offer protection and compensation should the former prove ineffective.

Insurers

Insurance began in classical Athens, and indeed was one of the institutional structures that allowed that city-state's economy to grow and

Table 4.1 Sample of terrorism insurance premiums (from a Lloyd's underwriter, interviewed from 23 April 2009)

Location	Terrorism Insurance Premium (% per annum)
North America	0.0152
Europe	0.0180
South Asia	0.0700
North Asia	0.0300
Australasia	0.0230

Source: Talas and Menachof (2014).

international trade to develop. The insurance in the Athenian case covered maritime cargoes. Today there is an extensive framework of private insurance institutions that are active in a variety of security areas for a price. And, as we can see from the very broad figures set out in Table 4.1, the fees that underwriters Lloyd's of London charge their clients in the port sector vary widely across geographical markets.

In terms of theory, economists have traditionally treated insurance as different from 'ordinary' goods or services in that it is not desired in itself to meet a basic need. Kenneth Arrow (1965), for example, argues that, 'Insurance is not a material good. . .its value to the buyer is clearly different in kind from the satisfaction of consumers' desires for medical treatment or transportation. Indeed, unlike goods or services, transactions involving insurance are an exchange of money for money, not money for something which directly meets needs.' This distinction, however, has been questioned more recently by the likes of Kelvin Lancaster (1966) and by Michael and Becker (1973), and the contemporary view is that the type of distinction drawn by Arrow is not relevant and that insurance can be treated, allowing for its particular features, as one would any other good or service. This reformation of theory is important and relevant to our discussions.

Insurance, and the markets in which it is traded, however, is still a complex matter. Private insurance only normally covers risk because of the need to be able to appraise actuarial risk when setting premiums. Besides the difficulties of estimating the level of risk, a major challenge confronting any insurer is that of moral hazard. This is essentially a situation where the insured party reduces its own security measures, knowing that any damage will be paid for by the insurance company, and ultimately by the other participants in the market through their premiums. Put simply, insurance may foster the insured to take excessive risks.[9]

Moral hazard may be seen as a special case of information asymmetry whereby one party in a transaction has more information than another. It is often found in situations where a party that is insulated from risk (the insured) has more information about its actions and intentions than the party paying for the negative consequences of the risk (the insurer). In these circumstances, the party with more information about its actions or intentions has an incentive to behave inappropriately from the perspective of the party with less information.

'Information' in the context of conventional insurance, as highlighted in Chapter 3, takes the form of estimating actuarial risk, something that we reemphasize is often not, or only partly, known in the context of security. With conventional insurance there is often a tendency for the suppliers of insurance to have more information than the insured about the risk of an event because of their past experiences and their in-house expertise. The latter, as a generalization, tend to be more risk averse and to over insure. Further, again because of their broad experience, insurers have considerable information on how to structure contracts so that the insured will not take on, from the insurer's perspective, excessive risk. There is no reason to assume transportation is different from other sectors in this respect.

In terms of terrorist attacks where the element of uncertainty is often dominant, one approach to insurance is to have the potential attackers insure you, the concept often known as 'protection money' to ensure a safe passage. The problems with this are numerous as an economic solution, and it is relatively easy to highlight the instability of the approach.

The taking of protection money (often called 'tribute' when states are concerned) by the Anglo-Saxons, Hengist and Horsa in the fifth century from Vortigern, King of the Britons, and their subsequent massacring of the Britons highlights a major defect of this type of 'insurance' arrangement (Bede, 741). The protectors have more information on their intentions than do the 'protected'; the former are also offering both the danger and, at a fee, the protection; a sort of two-sided market. There is also the problem for the protected that should the protector renege on an agreement after the 'tribute' has been paid there is little recourse for redeeming the payment, or indeed preventing the protector from pursuing its original aggressive policies.

Nevertheless, there are historic cases where the payment of protection money produced economic benefits, as Frederic Lane (1966) points out in the context of maritime trade in the eleventh century when Venice provided naval protection for the Byzantium Empire in exchange for trading privileges. In economic terms both parties gained from the transactions in the short term. The Venetians, being a near monopoly provider of naval protection services, could demand high economic rents from their services in terms of the trade that they conducted and the Empire avoided the need to build up its own navy. In the longer term the customer for naval services, the Byzantium Empire, however, was confronted by ever-increasing demands from the Venetian Doges.

Self-insurance and Self-protection

As alternatives to using the insurance market involve self-insurance – a reduction in the size of a loss – and self-protection – a reduction in the probability of a loss, although in some cases it is difficult to distinguish actions that reduce the probability of a loss from activity that reduces the size of a potential loss; many actions do both.[10] For example, our earlier case of a person riding 'shotgun' on a stagecoach epitomizes self-protection from attack. More modern versions may be seen in the armored trucks used to transport bank funds, and shipping companies' use of armed guards to combat the upsurge of piracy in the early 2000s. From the economics angle, the obvious problem with this is the potential escalation in costs that can occur as some form of arms race develops between the transporting companies and the attackers.

In a way self-protection may be treated as a means of self-insurance in that it either negates the need for insurance or reduces it. For this to be efficient, the cost of the protection must exceed the premium and other costs (such as searching for an insurer and waiting for recompense) of insurance. Again couched in terms of asymmetrical information, in this case the transportation undertaking assumes it is better informed of the particular risks confronting it than an insurance company. As with insurance, the element of uncertainty that is particularly associated with terrorist attacks is more difficult to handle.

Market insurance, public insurance, self-insurance and self-protection are not always independent, and there are generally interactions between them. Ehrlich and Becker (1972), for example, highlight these in terms of externalities. In the sense that those wishing to attack the transportation system are likely to seek easier targets, the adoption of self-protection by any party involved in the system will increase the chances of attack on other elements of the system; for example airports tightening their security may increase terrorists' attention on shopping malls or railways.

As with all externalities, the scope of the market must, however, be seen as relevant here, and some care is warranted. As Heal and Kunreuther (2005) explain, 'Any agent's incentive to adopt risk-reducing measures depends on the actions of others because of the negative externalities created by not investing in protection.' Looked at another way, a single airport tightening its own security may have potentially adverse effects on other airports if knowledge of this is advertised, by increasing their perceived relative vulnerability. But if a potential terrorist simply knows that one airport is now more secure, but not which one, the added security may de facto reduce the threat to the other airports and divert terrorist activity to transportation elsewhere, or some other target. There is thus a positive external effect across airports, but a negative external cost across the wider transportation system and other activities; see Ayres and Levitt (1998) for the relevant theory.

The implications of self-insurance vary because it has no impact on the targets selected by, say, terrorists; a terrorist is indifferent to attack in this context because each is equally vulnerable, it is just that the self-insured may be more resilient in terms of their ability to recover.

Public policies for handling these adverse external effects could theoretically involve Pigouvian subsidies and taxes within a traditional welfare economics framework. This would involve, for example, those adopting self-protection being taxed for the negative external costs they impose on others. Besides seeming counter-intuitive in that it encourages moral hazard, and thus is unlikely to be widely accepted, this approach would involve defining, measuring and monitoring self-protective actions, which is difficult.

One alternative is, given the high degree of substitutability between market and self-protection, for the government to subsidize the former to make it more attractive, or to provide public insurance, although again specifying exactly what this entails encounters definitional and measurement issues. Public protection through policing and intelligence is still another approach, and can have external benefits in deterring wider anti-social behavior.[11] In practice, policies generally entail combining public subsidization of insurance or its public provision, with public protection.

4.6 CONCLUSIONS

It is impossible to have an entirely secure world. There have always been, and will continue to be, groups and individuals that for a variety of reasons wish to disrupt the status quo with violent actions. This inevitably means disruption of market processes. But markets themselves exist because of their abilities to coordinate through automatic price mechanisms the preferences of various groups, including those concerned about their security. Thus market mechanisms, albeit often very imperfect in their nature, generally emerge to deal with the challenges posed by threats such as terrorists.

There are, for example, some circumstances where the private benefits of security act as an incentive for transportation companies to increase security activities and self-protect. This may be pronounced in situations where the market is characterized as an oligopoly, and where elements of quality competition, including that in security, are relevant, or with cartels, where internal pressures lead to collegiate pressures for common levels of security. Security is not costless, however, and, in general, transportation service suppliers require a degree of market power in order to be able to resource security measures. The challenge is that not only may this market power be undesirable in non-security ways, although this depends on the nature of the particular market involved, but it may directly lead to more attacks on softer elements in the supply chain.

NOTES

1. Pure public goods are non-excludable: you cannot stop people consuming them; and non-rival: one person's consumption does not adversely affect the consumption of others. With these features there is nothing to stop over-consumption, and no incentive, because they cannot be priced, for anyone to supply them in a market. In practice, pure public goods act more as a benchmark with the focus on whether goods or services have features approaching those of a pure public good.
2. A fuller account of the definition and the problems associated with public goods is contained in Holcombe (1997).
3. In line with domestic security in countries like the US where the poorer sections of society are most prone to attack, it is the poorer countries where overall security is most likely to be the major concern, and in many the annual death and injury tolls exceed the single attack on the US in 2001 many times over.
4. There may be a number of areas where there are synergies leading to both public and private benefits for transportation companies in adopting their own security measures; a Transportation Research Board (2003) study, for instance, focused on information systems.
5. Two good surveys setting out what we do know are found in Nicholas Economides (1996) and Oz Sly (2001).
6. The New Institutional Economics also tends to be more constructive in its orientation than traditional institutional economics, as epitomized in the works of Common, Veblen and Ayres, which often sought to discredit the paradigms of neoclassical economics without really establishing a firm edifice to replace them.
7. This topic is dealt with in more detail in the context of maritime security in Brooks and Button (2006).
8. While these are treated here as commercial entities functioning in the free insurance market, in countries like Israel and the UK there is also formal government participation in terrorist coverage.
9. Much of the modern economic analysis of moral hazard issues can be traced back to Kenneth Arrow (1963). For a counter-argument to the moral hazard position, see Ehrlich and Becker (1972).
10. The terms 'loss protection' and 'loss prevention' are also sometimes used.
11. While the Ehrlich and Becker (1972) analysis is in terms of private goods and externalities, an alternative approach is to think of self-insurance and self-protection in terms of them being public goods; for example see Lohse et al. (2012). In this case, something like 'policing' of the seas off Somalia may be seen as a local public good that acts as insurance against attack by pirates. Because such public goods are known to those who may otherwise self-insure (or not), this removes the moral hazard problem.

5. The economic instruments of security policy

We will bankrupt ourselves in the vain search for absolute security
Dwight D. Eisenhower

5.1 INTRODUCTION

Harry H. Truman, the post-Second World War President of the United States, had a plaque on his desk highlighting that the 'Buck Stops Here'. This signified that the responsibilities of government, as personified by the President in this context, are extensive. At a more detailed, economic level it also confirms that government determines the parameters of markets, and whether markets should indeed be the main mechanisms for resource, including security, allocation.[1] Essentially all markets for security, as we have seen, function within institutional boundaries, and in addition to this there are numerous command-and-control mechanisms that government can use to influence security resource use and allocation.

There are two broad stereotyped approaches to economic regulation. The Anglo-Saxon approach considers that market forces are largely the best way of meeting economic efficiency objectives and that interventions are only justified if it can be demonstrated that they produce a superior outcome. Simply showing that any market for security does not work efficiently, under this scenario, is in itself not a justification for regulation or government provision. At the other extreme is the Continental philosophy that argues for government control unless the market can clearly provide a better outcome. The differences are manifestly to do with burden of proof. In practice, countries never follow the extremes of these approaches; even regimes such as North Korea have some elements of markets in their systems, but it is a matter of degree.

The relevance for this from a security perspective is in terms of deciding who is responsible for providing security. At one level this is a matter of whether security should largely be driven by the market or through regulation. There is no self-evident answer to this, or at least not in many cases, and much would seem to depend on the nature and context of the issue at hand. There are also different philosophies. For example, the Second Amendment of the Constitution of the US upholds the right of citizens to bear arms,[2] highlighting the role of the individual to protect his/her security, whereas in countries like the UK there is a much greater burden placed on the national government. But in addition, and the issue examined in this chapter, there are second tier questions regarding just how the government should act when it does intervene; amongst other things, what tools should it use, how should they be used, and how should they be evaluated? There are the associated questions of who are the best people to use these tools, essentially questions of degrees of outsourcing when it comes to the role of private companies.

5.2 ECONOMICS AND INSTITUTIONS

Oliver Williamson (2000) opens his wider-ranging survey of the New Institutional Economics (NIE), cited in Chapter 4, by admitting that considerable ignorance still exists about institutions, their form and their interactions, and further admits that study of institutions is still at a stage of looking at partial mechanisms rather than the generation of general theories. Nevertheless, the thrust of his argument is that using what we do know is better than ignoring institutions or treating them in an excessively simplistic manner.

New Institutional Economics

The modern institutional economic theorists reject the two central ideas of neoclassical theory – costless transactions and neutral institutions.[3] They embrace the notion that the norm is for there to be positive transaction costs, and view institutions as influencing these transaction costs and individuals' incentives, and thus their economic behavior. Because of transaction costs, the neoclassical view of perfect rationality has to be replaced by some version of 'bounded rationality' and 'satisficing' (Simon, 1955); essentially, decision-makers operate with incomplete knowledge, and do not try to optimize decisions but look for acceptable outcomes. Further, these theorists elaborate on the concept of transaction costs and related notions, and view institutions as endogenous variables in the economic models that emerge and as a consequence of economic motivations as well as external shocks to the system.

As we saw in Figure 4.1, the new institutional approach sets neoclassical economics and conventional neoclassical views of markets within a larger framework that considers not only the immediacy of markets but also the institutional context, both formal and informal, in which markets function. As that figure also suggested, there can be rigidity in the system and it may take years for change to occur within the various elements. In some cases, such as legal reforms, the formal wheels of government have to react, and this can be a slow process where there are established constitutions and protocols to follow. Social change, for example, can take generations because of inertia and reluctance to experiment with new social orders.

Transaction Costs

The perception, if not always the actuality, of the nature and scale of transaction costs is at the core of many of the decisions regarding the need for government oversight of transportation security, and deserves a fuller discussion.

While most of the microeconomic issues addressed today focus on immediate resource allocation, the clearing of markets, and, in particular, on price formulation, in the somewhat longer term there emerge transaction cost considerations. Williamson's (1985) definition of a transaction is when 'a good or service is transferred across a technologically separable surface as one stage of activity terminates and another begins'. Transactions occur among a variety of economic actors: researchers, capitalists, manufacturers, labor, suppliers of raw materials and intermediate products, and others who jointly address problems such as raising capital, deciding on product standards, setting levels of output, wages and prices, and marketing products to consumers; all things that have to be embraced when considering security provision. These are preconditions to what are normally seen as the workings of the ongoing market and to the extent of markets. For example, they determine the extent to which markets coordinate production (that is, price transactions between firms) and the degree to which coordination comes through management (that is, non-price transactions within firms).

Economic and 'political' costs are involved in these transactions. The former pertain to market transaction costs and the costs to the authority of issuing, monitoring and enforcing orders inside a firm (that is, managerial transaction costs). The use of the market involves deciding with whom to negotiate and sign a contract, and later to monitor contract performance. Ronald Coase (1960) recognizes three types of such costs: search and information – contract preparation costs, bargaining and decision-making; contract conclusion costs; and contract monitoring and enforcement costs. Managerial transaction costs involve the costs of setting up, maintaining and changing a firm, and the costs of running it.

Political transaction costs arise because economic, market and managerial transactions can occur only in the context of political institutional arrangements consistent with a capitalist market environment. This implies the need for some form of organization with associated public goods and costs.[4] The costs of supplying goods by collective action are political transaction costs that comprise the costs of setting up, maintaining and changing the background formal and informal political organizations, and the costs of running the polity. There are inevitable political outlays associated with this, and retaining public support for particular actions inevitably leads to a degree of Tullock rent-seeking loss; basically, non-productive activities aimed solely at transferring support away from other groups.

These transaction costs have to be incurred to facilitate orderly transfers of property rights in economic transactions. Broadly stated, such costs can be viewed as the costs of specialization and division of labor. Further, their level can vary with the nature of the broader society and the constituent individual behavior. If there were greater trust and shared norms or mental models among individuals, monitoring and enforcement costs could be lower – suggesting interrelationships between trust, social values and institutional frameworks. If we just take the air transport industry, the growth of such features as various types of legal protection of 'consumer rights' in the European Union regarding such things as compensation for lost baggage, delayed flights or being 'bumped' off a flight suggests trust between passengers and airlines is hardly growing.

In addition to the concept of transaction costs associated with the exchange process, modern institutional economics utilizes two other analytical constructs to support insights: those pertaining to the analysis of property rights and the economic theory of contracts.

The right of ownership of an asset consists of the rights to use it, to change its form and substance, and to transfer some or all rights as desired. The assumption is that property rights are assigned according to the principle of private ownership, giving the individual discretionary power over resources and providing a basis for competitive markets. In a world with positive and ubiquitous transaction costs, uncertainty and asymmetric information prevail. Under these circumstances, the pattern of property rights and the mechanisms by which they may be traded in an economy affect economic incentives and thus behavior and economic outcomes.

A major area of concern is the economic theory of contracts. The NIE formally approaches transaction costs by analysing their effects, starting with situations when they are high, when it is either too costly or impossible to find out about future conditions, and there is asymmetric information. Imperfect foresight prevents the preparation of a contract that embraces all conceivable contingencies in the future, and may make it difficult for contract enforcement – thus leaving gaps in contracts and room for later adjustment. Such issues are addressed by incomplete contract theory. Asymmetric information typically occurs in the principal–agent case when an agent (for example an employee) enjoys an informational advantage over the principal (for example a firm owner). Such occurrence is observed in two contexts: pre-contractual asymmetric information (adverse selection), and post-contractual asymmetrical information (moral hazard) – with the better-informed party potentially engaging in opportunism.

The overall insight is that several economic coordinating mechanisms, or institutions, can emerge in economies. The emergence of these various institutional types depends on the circumstances prevailing in an economy and the degree to which these circumstances are consistent with the inherent logic of a particular institutional mechanism. Further, there are arguments that the different institutions of capitalism complement one another and cannot generally function in isolation from one another (Baumol et al., 2007).

In many countries there is currently a widespread view that the most efficient institution for coordination of economic activity is the 'market'. The neoclassical framework underlying this view is rationalistic, individualistic and utilitarian. In the traditional version, market coordination occurs when economic actors remain autonomous, pursue their interests vigorously and engage in decentralized arm's-length bargaining. These economic actors indicate their preferences and prices through relatively comprehensive contracts, which are self-liquidating with completion of contract performance – without requiring further interactions among economic actors (Williamson, 1985). The objective is to complete on-the-spot, instantaneous transactions without any implications for future activities or strategies. This is clearly a stylized characterization of the classical market – pure competitive spot markets – however, one can recognize a large number of variants and modifications of this form.

Economists in this tradition hold an adverse view of other institutional mechanisms for economic coordination. In their view, most alternative institutional forms and the state generally do more harm than good. In spite of this, however, the new economic institutionalists do not view the market as always the ideal and universal arrangement for coordinating economic activities. When efforts are made to organize economic activities exclusively in terms of markets, they can function well and provide social optima only if some structural conditions obtain in the larger economy. Such conditions include: absence of uncertainty, reversibility of transactions, completely contingent markets, non-occurrence of increasing returns to scale, and no collusion among economic actors. Adam Smith's invisible hand solution applies under these circumstances. More generally, we can state that the organization of the economy solely in terms of markets generates several types of inefficiencies and drawbacks in economic coordination. These are the sorts of problems highlighted by those supporting more widespread actions by government to ensure security in society.

Some economists highlight the first deficiency and argue that private hierarchical organizations, such as firms, are more efficient under certain conditions than markets and inter-firm contracts (Coase, 1937). When economic actors carry out their transactions within a firm or a private hierarchy, they can often reduce transaction costs, enhance efficiency and reduce the opportunism inherent in exchange relationships. The incentives to realize lower production costs and greater scale economies promote economic agents to act within firms rather than outside the firm. This process of internalizing economic transactions inside a firm lowers risk and uncertainty and confers the capability of achieving lower costs and higher levels of productivity, in the context of large markets and capital-intensive but fairly stable technologies.

While markets exhibit strengths in the efficient provision of private and divisible goods, they evidence weaknesses requiring supplementary support in two broad areas.

- First, state intervention is generally required as a minimum to enforce the rules among interacting economic agents. Such institutional arrangements pertain to the supply of public goods for collective action. Such goods relate to the creation and maintenance of legal, judicial and administrative frameworks for facilitating economic transactions, and the process of running such a polity. The provision of such organizations is the province of the state as an institution. The state sanctions and regulates other non-state coordinating mechanisms, and is the ultimate enforcer of the rules of other mechanisms that enumerate and enforce property rights and set monetary and fiscal policy. By offering such an organizational apparatus related to contract enforcement, property rights transfer and so on, the state facilitates economic transactions in the market and among firms – a role acknowledged by Adam Smith.
- A second argument for the state as an economic institution derives from the notion of market failure when markets result in problems associated with public goods, market instability and so on.[5] During the 1930s and 1940s, a variety of perceived market failures led to state intervention in the form of extensive regulation and monitoring and guiding of transportation activities. Recent theoretical developments suggest that modern industrialized economies are unable to realize their potential for economic growth and development without

market interventions; ensuring sustainable environments and social structures are generally seen as examples. When negative externalities occur because of excessive costs involved in adequately allocating and enforcing property rights, there is the case for the state to provide economic coordination mechanisms if it can demonstrate that these can perform better than imperfect markets. If clean air or water or airspace are viewed as free goods, households and firms have little incentive for preserving the environment or quality of airspace. By creating environmental standards and mechanisms for allocating polluting rights or flying rights (a quasi-market mechanism) state institutions may be able to support more efficient economic transactions.[6]

Table 5.1 displays the differentiating attributes of the three basic institutions under which transportation services are supplied – markets, firms and the state – and highlights some of the strengths and weaknesses of each.

Table 5.1 Differentiating characteristics of basic economic institutions

Institutional Characteristics	Market	Private Hierarchies	State
Organizational Attributes	Free entry and exit Voluntary spot exchanges	Bureaucratic rules and trends Exchange based on asymmetric power	Public hierarchy unilateral action
Compliance Mechanisms	Legal enforcement Private property	Institutional rules Corporate culture	Coercion Social rules and norms
Institutional Failure			
Enforcement	Collusion Imperfect competition	Opportunistic behavior	'Public Failure' Lobbies capturing public interest objectives
Public goods and externalities	Inability to produce public goods Difficulties in adapting to technical change and innovation	Slow reaction to technological change	Can provide public goods, but 'in what quantities?' Difficulty in inducing technical change
Efficiency	Some basic social relations not producible by pure market	Difficulties in adapting to cooperative behavior	Bureaucratic ambience Higher cost of services
Equity	Promotion of income and wealth inequalities	Management overload and inequality	Power and privilege may enhance inequality

Source: Based on Hollingsworth and Boyer (1997) and Furubotn and Richter (1997).

What may be important in a transportation security context are the factors that bring about the adoption of particular institutional structures, and why they may change or adjust over time. Douglass North (1994) views institutional change as being triggered mainly by changes in relative prices, or in individual preferences; in the latter case a major attack on the transportation network, of which 11 September 2001 was a clear example. Prices in this context embrace costs of market transactions, the costs of acquisition of technologies or competences, and relative factor prices. Such price changes flow from activities of the innovation-creator and the entrepreneur, who shape the nature and direction of competences that economic actors need. North suggests that adaptive change on the part of the economic actor arises in this context, and this activates the mechanisms of institutional change. An example of this in the transportation context would be the emergence of a new fingerprint or cornea identification technology that fosters changes in legal security requirements at airport checkpoints.

Thus existing institutions are buffeted, shaped and reshaped by historical and emerging changes in technology and markets and the consequent evolving nature of economic interactions in society. Such emerging changes in economic interaction patterns represent and simultaneously provide arenas for experiments, trial and error processes, and learning among economic agents at the micro level and potentially at the macro institutional level. In this case, the gap or mismatches in the incentives at the micro and macro institutional levels are the driving forces behind institutional change. The rise of the knowledge economy in recent years and its predominant spatial location in a number of dynamic regional economies in North America, Europe and Asia, is often cited as offering such a context of major technical and market evolution and the consequent modification in the nature and structure of incentives for economic actors – a fertile ground for the reform and evolution of new institutions. A similar argument can be made for the developments in security technology that have often emanated from particular sectors such as transportation.

5.3 THE NATURE OF POLICY RESPONSES

Anti-terrorism activities generally fall under three broad umbrellas: the initial prevention and deterrence of an incident; the short-term response to an incident and crisis management; and the longer-term remediation and recovery from an incident when one does occur.

Historically, what have largely been missing are efforts to optimize across all three levels of security: prevention, resilience and recovery. Instead, piecemeal approaches tend to be the norm, with particular emphasis on one of the levels. It appears that much of the earlier focus after 11 September 2001 was, for example, on the first of these. To quote Henry Willis and David Ortiz (2004),

> Both public and private sector initiatives to improve the security of the global supply chain have focused largely on preventing and deterring smuggling and terrorist attacks. . . Few initiatives have focused on improving the fault tolerance or resilience of the system, which could be a fruitful area for new security measures.

The trend more recently, however, as seen in the survey by Julie Gould et al. (2010), has been to give more emphasis to the resilience of the transportation system to attack. This involves both what may be seen as negative resilience: the ability of the system to withstand an assault, essentially flexibility, and positive resilience: the ability to recover rapidly.

Within these categories of response, and overlapping with them, there is a further subdivision in terms of the economic ethos that underlay the policies adopted: basically are they supply or demand driven?

The conventional approach, or at least the one that tends to get highlighted, involves making it more expensive for the potential perpetrators of terrorism to pursue their activities. In the transportation case, this may involve introducing security guards on ships, the introduction of explosive detecting equipment, the use of armored doors to the cockpits of commercial aircraft, the use of surveillance equipment at stations (Priks, 2015), and so on. Basically, this approach makes the tasks of the terrorists more difficult, and pushes up the costs of their achieving their aims.

In analytical terms, assuming terrorists have constrained resources, as indicated by the solid budget constraint curves in the upper part of Figure 5.1, then the higher marginal costs of committing terrorist acts push the constraint to the left and terrorist acts fall from T_1 to T_2. Given the changes in the relative costs of terrorism versus other, presumably less violent ways of seeking to achieve objectives, combined with the income effect that the actual acts of violence that still occur are now more costly, the trend will be for pursuing more peaceful initiatives (O_1 to O_2 in Figure 5.1).

The alternative approach is to lessen the impacts of terrorist acts and thus reduce their perceived benefits to terrorists. This may be achieved by, for instance, spreading out the vulnerable points in a transportation network, say by having fewer and smaller shopping malls or airport terminals, making cargo holds on aircraft more bomb resistant, or not publicizing the name of the perpetrator. In this case, the benefit gained from each act of terrorism to terrorists is reduced, pulling to the left their utility curve from such actions (bottom of Figure 5.1). Again terrorism is reduced.

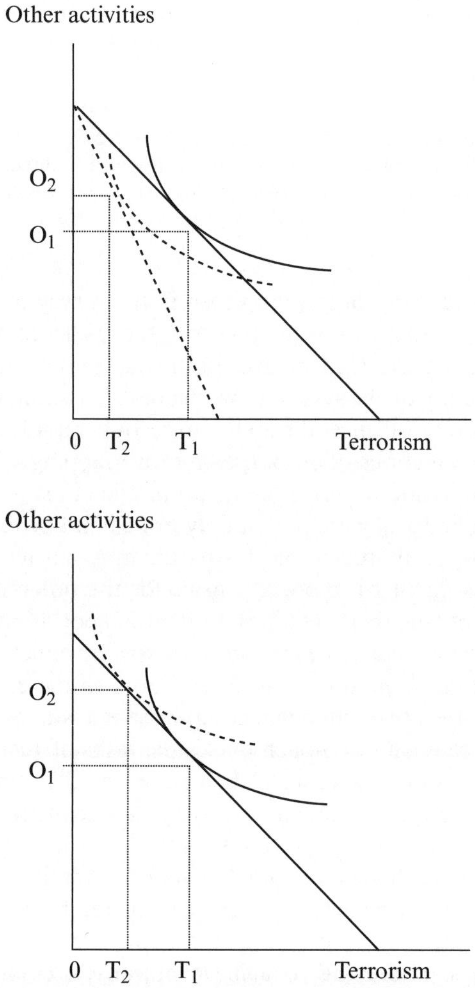

Figure 5.1 *The effects on terrorism of increasing the marginal costs to terrorists (top) and of reducing the marginal benefits from their actions (bottom)*

A twist on this dichotomy is provided by Bruno Frey and Simon Luechinger (2003) who, instead of focusing on increasing the marginal costs incurred by terrorists or on reducing the impacts of their actions, both measures basically designed to increase resilience, they consider the case of making the alternative to terrorism more attractive.

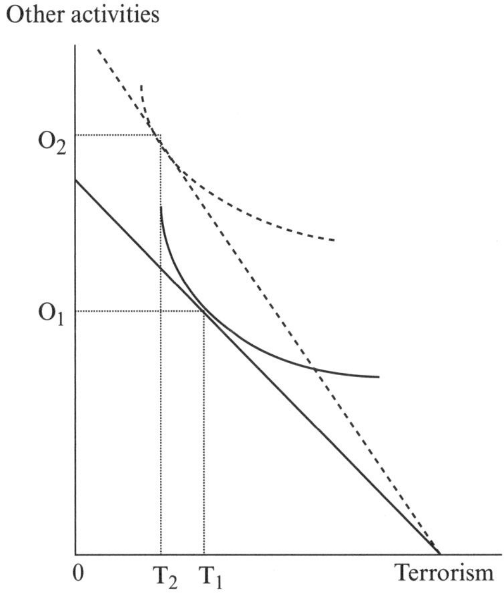

Figure 5.2 Making non-terrorist actions more attractive

Figure 5.2 illustrates this sort of situation, with the original budget line shifting out and the level of terrorism falling from T_1 to T_2. Whether the outcome is more or less terrorist activity is an empirical one in this case. It is quite possible, for example, that because of the higher real income going to potential terrorists as a result of making other activities cheaper, a large part of this may be used to finance more terrorist activities as well as for the purchase of other activities, despite the changes in their relative prices. In other words, the new indifference curve hits the new budget line at a point leading to terrorism to the right of T_1, rather than to the left as drawn. It all depends on the nature of the indifference curve mapping.

But is this type of approach realistic? A situation of this kind may, at least in part, explain the decline in piracy off the Somalia coast from 2011 as local fishermen have been afforded more protection for their fishing grounds and more local jobs created, although separating this enhanced protection for merchant ships is difficult. There is also the challenge in this sort of approach that terrorists, if they anticipate this sort of policy approach, will simply be aggressive to obtain concessions in the form of 'other goods' that essentially meet their objective. The Somalia case may be thought of in these terms. Part of the motivation for the piracy was initiated when fishermen began losing their livelihood as a result of illegal foreign fishing vessels operating in their waters. Illegal fishing fell after international intervention to stop the piracy.

Deciding on the best economic approach selecting from these policy approaches normally involves applying some form of quasi-cost–benefit or cost-effectiveness analysis. As we have seen in Chapter 3, this is not easy to do and is normally a matter of looking at particular cases. But even then, as we have seen, this is difficult because terrorism involves not only uncertainty, because of the limited number of previous events and the game playing by perpetrators, but lack of clarity, especially *ex ante*, in the objectives of terrorists and the potential wide-ranging implications of their actions. To get a broad handle on the shapes of the curves seen in Figures 5.1 and 5.2, perhaps the best tools available are experiments. These may involve some form of conventional simulations that can help assess static uncertainty, or more interactive approaches deploying experimental economics that can capture the adaptive behavior of terrorists to security measures.

While it is generally impossible to identify and quantify many of the costs and benefits of securing transportation facilities, there are important questions about who should pay the costs if the terrorist threat is to be handled efficiently. All the options we have outlined have opportunity costs to society; there is no win–win situation, or at least it is difficult to envisage one.

More generally, while useful, this type of risk analysis has limitations when dealing with terrorism. Essentially, the difficulty is that the benefit curve of additional security cannot be estimated in actuarial terms; it is about uncertainty and it is seldom about marginalism. A common approach to dealing with this type of uncertainty problem is to seek out situations of vulnerability and develop strategies that can reduce this vulnerability, or that may provide flexibility if there are attacks on vulnerable points. A significant degree of subjectivity and 'expert opinion' is inevitably involved, and it is almost impossible to judge success. Containers, for example, because of their number, nature and continual motion would seem to be a vulnerable link in the security network although they have not yet been widely used as a medium of attack. Their visibility adds to the public perception of vulnerability. Reducing this vulnerability, real or otherwise, is costly; physical searches of every container take up people's time, manpower and equipment.

In practical terms, since industry will inevitably bear much of the immediate incidence of security actions, it is important to understand the underlying market structure of the sector affected if costs are to be optimized. The effectiveness and costs of any security regime involving transportation undertakings are certainly not independent of the form of the particular subsector of the industry involved. The adoption of measures to reduce vulnerability inevitably entails official regulations and controls, but also may embody actions by those in the larger supply chain in response to commercial considerations. From a policy perspective, authorities require fairly good information therefore, not only on the reactions of those involved in the particular transportation industry to legal requirements but also as to the extent and nature of any internal market reaction to security threats. The nature of the market largely determines both forms of reaction.

To retain public confidence in transportation as an integral part of the social and economic fabric of a country, there is a need to ensure that the dangers of a terrorist attack are kept within acceptable limits. What 'acceptable' implies is largely a political matter, but there are also clear issues about the best ways of achieving any level of acceptable security in a purely technical sense; for example, what should be the role of technology and what form should it take? But there are also more basic issues of the roles of the various interested parties in achieving optimal levels of security, and this is where market structures can be important.

In abstract, but hopefully simple, terms the actors involved can be broken down into those with a private incentive to ensure appropriate security of transportation, and those that have a more indirect social motive in wanting to serve the 'public interest'. The security goals of these two groups generally diverge. The first group, driven by Adam Smith's invisible hand, will react to the profit motive and ensure investment in security that is consistent with it maximizing the net income of those that compose it. The second group will be more inclined to see numerous market failures that allow security issues to slip through the fingers of the invisible hand and result in a socially inadequate level of security. They will favor public measures and possibly public expenditure to combat these failures.

In practice, there is a de facto deployment of both the commercial and public interest views of security in the ways in which strategies are developed. The balance is often determined implicitly by a weighing up of several factors (O'Hanlon et al., 2002). The extent to which the public and private sectors act rationally in response to risks does not always appear to be related to information before them. For example, many members of the public perceive airline travel to be more dangerous than driving a car, whereas equally they very well know that statistics show the opposite.

5.4 THE TOOLKIT OF ECONOMIC INSTRUMENTS

We do not dwell on the details of every instrument of the security toolkit of economic measures available, but rather provide some broad guidelines

Table 5.2 Taxonomy of the instruments available to help secure transportation systems

	Market-based incentives		Command-and-control instruments	
	Direct	Indirect	Direct	Indirect
Infrastructure	Subsidies to public goods Legal liability	Public–private partnerships	Design standards Access inspections Access barriers Neutralizing zones Integrated planning	Intelligence Emergency response services Policing
Operations	Legal liability	Taxes on self-insurance Taxes on self-protection	Operator licenses Preferred suppliers Customer/cargo checks Directed routing	Policing/monitoring Emergency response services Information/communication Policing
Vehicles	Subsidies Security R&D support		Design features On-board security devices	Driver checks Operational controls

as to their nature and limitations. The rationale for this is quite simply that the usefulness of various instruments is generally contextual and, in particular, in the case of transportation tends to be mode and location specific and aligned to the types of transportation being considered. Table 5.2, however, offers a very rough and ready overview of the types of policy tools available, categorized by whether they apply largely to transportation infrastructures, operations, or the 'vehicles' used, and whether the instruments can be seen as essentially market based or a command-and-control type. There is an inevitable subjectivity in producing this taxonomy, and some instruments depending on how they are deployed may well fit into several categories.

While some of the instruments have a manifest economic component, even those of a harder, command-and-control nature have economic implications. There are the immediate costs of implementation of the various forms of control that not only vary in level but also differ regarding where the ultimate incidents lie; for example the burden borne by the supplier of transportation services and that on the user. The nature of the transportation market as seen earlier in Chapter 4 has relevance in this regard.

The reason why there are public policy initiatives to handle transportation security is, to reemphasize, the result of various market failures, including those associated with who carries the burden of paying for security. The market-based instruments, both those directly affecting security or those indirectly doing so through other markets such as insurance, may be seen as one way of internalizing externalities or providing public goods to compensate for these failures. Some of these, such as liability allocation, take a quasi-Coasian approach, while taxes on self-insurance, as we saw in the previous chapter, are more of a Pigouvian nature.

The direct regulation of security comes in a diversity of forms. At one extreme, the government takes direct responsibility for providing security, be it at the micro, meso or macroeconomic level, while at the other it may involve some general oversight of the performance of private sector security suppliers or the operations of the internal security measures of individual transportation suppliers. But within these groups there is much devolution of authority to agencies and other bodies to allow for particular local or industrial peculiarities. Similarly, the details of the instruments used vary, largely by mode and context.

In terms of selecting policy instruments, besides efficiency, and especially transaction costs, the political economy of who bears the burden of the incidence of the costs of adequate security is important. Clearly many groups may be affected, depending on the portfolio of instruments that are adopted. How the various affected parties are defined is a clear problem here and generally involves normative decisions regarding impacts on various income groups and the various categories of transportation user. But taking the simplest breakdown that divides the world into transportation user and transportation supplier, the relevance of demand conditions becomes apparent in Figure 5.3.

Whichever instrument is used, be it a tax or regulation, it will push up the costs of transportation, thus causing the cost curve to move up from $Cost_1$ to $Cost_2$. If a direct subsidy is involved to pay for additional security then the taxpayer may be seen as the de facto user of transportation. The two shaded areas represent the incidence of this cost on the users and suppliers of transportation. While the absolute costs are determined by the elasticity of demand, the shares respectively borne by the users and the suppliers of transportation are determined by the slope of the demand curve: the steeper it is the more that the user will bear; the darker-shaded area increases and the lighter-shaded area shrinks. This

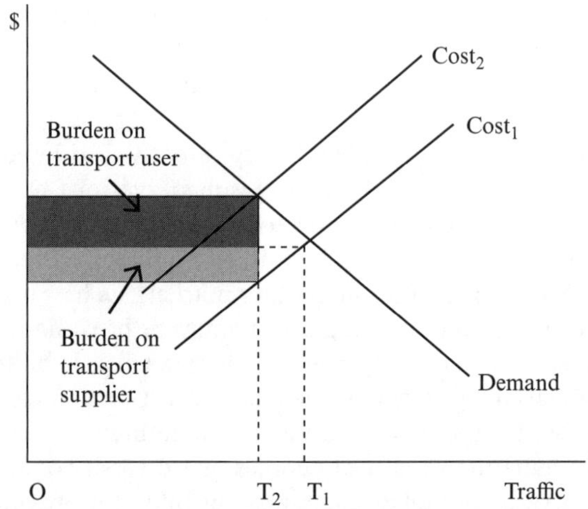

Figure 5.3 The incidence of the costs of security measures

has particular implications when the demand curve is steep, and the users are, for example, low-income groups. In this case a Pigouvian subsidy, for example, may be deemed more socially and politically accepted than a tax.

5.5 PUBLIC–PRIVATE PARTNERSHIPS

Public–private partnerships (PPPs) involve voluntary contractual agreements of public agencies and private companies to jointly finance a venture. In our case this would be investments or operations with enhanced security as the objective. They are widely used and increasingly common in the transportation sector more generally, although perhaps less so in the context of security (Button, 2016). The use of private security firms that tender for public sector contracts is one example. It should be distinguished from private sector subcontracting (also often called outsourcing), which is discussed in more detail later. One form of a PPP may involve the public sector using a private provider to meet a social objective. This differs from what we call subcontracting, when a commercial company, rather than providing security itself, buys in outside services as many shopping malls and warehouses do, or indeed the stagecoach operators in our earlier discussions used to do.

Innovations in private finance, problems with public acceptance of high taxation and concerns over the accountability of government agencies, have to some extent stimulated this trend. As Luc Leruth (2012) says, however, 'There has not been much economic theory specifically devoted to public–private ventures, but it is clear that the general frameworks of contract theory, risk analysis, project financing, the theory of incentives, and others directly apply.'

There has also not been overall agreement on the general desirability of PPPs and on the success of those that have been implemented. From the private enterprise perspective, PPPs can be seen as opening up business opportunities previously the preserve of the public sector. But there are practical issues concerning contract design and accountability, and, when large investments are involved in, say, screening technology, the difficulty of handling transaction costs.

While there are variations, typically a PPP involves a government signing an agreement for a private company to supply services with the private sector actor designing, building, owning and running the physical assets, although not all components may be devolved. Basically a PPP is a long-term development and service contract between government and a private partner, with the latter getting its revenue directly from user fee or, and more common in the security context, indirectly through government payments. Virtually all forms of economic activity involve a degree of public–private cooperation because property rights, in all but the most totalitarian regimes, are shared between the two parties. The notion of public–private partnerships in the way the term is now commonly used, represents a general shift with the two parties changing in their roles in the provision of security services involving direct financial contracts, rather than direction by the government, being at the core.

There are inevitable challenges in reaching a viable partnership in this bilateral monopolistic/oligopolistic world of joint ventures. The focus here is very much on the economic dimensions of PPPs, which is not to say that there are not significant challenges regarding such things as political acceptability, management practices, and accountability.

An example of public sector engagement with the private involved in airport screening is the situation in the US after 11 September 2011. The political issue involved the general favoring of direct government provision by the Democratic Party and the use of franchising to the private sector by the Republicans. The Aviation and Transportation Security Act took over passenger and baggage screening at airports, most of which are state or metropolitan owned using a new federal workforce, but, under the Screening Partnership Program (SPP), it permitted five to use TSA-certified security firms. All airports were to be given this option after 2004. In January 2011 the TSA rejected pending applications for the SPP and announced that no more airports could participate. This was reversed after Senate intervention. In terms of the effectiveness of the private screening, the US Government Accountability Office (2009) found that, '. . .screening at SPP airports currently costs approximately 17.4% more to operate than at airports with federal screeners, and that SPP airports fell within the "average performer" category for the performance measures included in its analysis.' A US House Committee on Transportation and Infrastructure (2011) study, however, found that Los Angeles TSA screeners only handled 9765 passengers an hour whereas San Francisco's contract screeners handled 16 000, despite similar pay scales and equipment.

An important distinction is found in the perspective of (a) private companies, such as ports and shopping malls, which are stockholders whose owners invest their own resources in security, and (b) public agencies that represent stakeholders that not only finance part of the system but also are affected by its larger outcomes. The former group focuses primarily on commercial criteria and the financial returns that an investment can generate, while the public sector's concern is with wider social criteria. In welfare economic terms, a profit maximizing private investor is only interested in 'producer surplus', the difference between money paid out to make the investment and the subsequent revenue earned, whereas the broader approach takes account of both the 'producer surplus' and the 'consumer surplus', basically a cost–benefit analysis (CBA) approach of the type discussed earlier.

There are differences in these approaches when trying to develop PPP frameworks for security provision. Besides taking a wider view of costs and benefits, an agency using CBA also takes a longer view than a private company using financial criteria. While the notion of discounting is inherent in both, the details of the calculations thus differ significantly, often leading to little common ground when public and private actors try to coordinate actions. Further, CBA often redefines many of the items retained from commercial criteria. One example is that the shadow price of labor, such as baggage inspectors at airports, that is used by commercially driven agencies involves taking the prevailing wage rate as the price, whereas, when there is unemployment, a public agency may take a lower wage to reflect the social benefits of job creation. The risk premiums in terms of the probability that the expenditures generate the expected benefits also vary. The private sector has only recourse to its own resources, whereas the public sector can cover losses by recourse to the national financial system; put simply, the taxpayer assumes at least part of the risk as we see in Chapter 6 regarding airport security in the United States. Finally, a commercial supplier will seek user fees that maximize returns, which may include price discrimination but with all users covering marginal cost, whereas a public agency may price to favor particular groups of potential users for social reasons, for example subsidizing the security costs of smaller airports in areas of high unemployment.

There are also some more practical issues to consider.

There are few independent elements of security infrastructure and their operation, but there are also often interdependencies between them. For example, at airports there are electronic scanners but these need manual operators. At its simplest, more investment costs also often mean lower labor costs, as seen in the relative costs of manual and electronic inspections of containers or airline passengers' luggage. The decisions regarding the optimal approach in such cases have as much to do with the inherent nature of transaction costs within the undertaking involved as they do with their method of provision. It is essentially a practical matter. If there are managerial synergies or high costs of unplanned coordination, then there are arguments for grouping activities in a PPP arrangement. The transaction costs of many stand-alone entities are higher than those when they are bundled.

The nature of contracts when there are externalities is also partly a matter of practicality; it is often, for example, relatively easy to specify a contract for an investment, such as for electronic container screening technology, but more difficult to specify a contract for its use or the labor force to be combined with it. In these cases unbundling is generally more efficient, with the public sector involved in the operation of the facility after a private sector builds it; Hart (2008) provides a theoretical underpinning for this. Essentially, if it is easy to clearly define the building criteria, but not the quality of the subsequent services generated, then unbundling, with the private sector providing the investment and leaving operations to the public, can be shown not to lead to any serious under-provision of effective security infrastructure. This is a more likely scenario than the reverse situation where the private sector is better informed about security operations and the public agency about infrastructure needs.

From a slightly different perspective, Oliver Hart et al. (1997) make a distinction between contracting out, which we look at below, and competitive tending under which public sector agencies may bid. The issue is thus about residual control rights that cannot be contracted out, and leads to a division between situations where contracting out is preferable. Basically, it is argued that private providers have a stronger incentive to engage in both quality improvement and cost reduction when providing security than a government agency, with the former's incentive to engage in cost reduction being typically much stronger because it ignores the adverse effect on service quality that is difficult to define in contracts.

Virtually all PPPs involve a large degree of bilateral oligopoly, and often, when highly specialized actions are concerned, bilateral monopoly.

Basically, to provide airport security a private company has to be of some size. Given the nature of government, ultimately property rights are in the hands of the public sector because, as the Public Choice School of economics emphasizes, all decisions are essentially political in the sense that governments set the rules for security contracts. In game theoretical jargon, the government is the principal and the private supplier the agent. In terms of large-scale investments, and the limited number of private sector investors capable of financing such projects, the negotiations underlying a PPP involve the exercise of market power. Conventional, neoclassical economic ideas of competitive equilibrium and the like do not apply, the outcome of a bilateral monopoly or oligopoly situation being normally indeterminate, depending on the bargaining skills of the parties involved. This makes PPPs difficult to form in any context, and not just regarding transportation security.

Globally, the experience is that many PPPs, irrespective of what they involve, are subsequently renegotiated.[7] There are often quite legitimate reasons why a PPP breaks down once physical construction or operations commenced, including unexpected rises in costs, the encountering of unforeseen technical problems, or changes in the security situation, basically rendering the initial contract incomplete as defined by Hart and Moore (1988). There is no reason to expect this to be different in the particular case of transportation security.

In these cases there are often justifications put forward for continuing with the existing actions of PPP partners; these may be couched in terms of equipment costs being bygones-being-bygones, the marginal gains to both parties of the additional costs not being justified, or because of high transaction costs in seeking new partners to continue the work after relationship-specific investments have been made. In other cases, however, a private contract may make a low offer to bid for the security work with the expectation that it can subsequently renegotiate; the lack of viable competitors or high fixed costs may stimulate this. The challenge is to find the appropriate level of flexibility: too much, and undesirable opportunistic renegotiations are likely to be necessary; too little, and opportunities for welfare-enhancing renegotiations will be lost. But, given the nature of risk and uncertainty, defining comprehensive contracts that allow for all contingencies is almost impossible, and incomplete contracts seem inevitable (Coase, 1937).

The operation and use of any security infrastructure, once completed, requires monitoring and, in most cases, regulating to ensure that contractual terms are met in the context of changing conditions, maintenance and the like (Laffont and Tirole, 1993). It also needed to ensure, from the public sector side, that the consumer surplus benefits are not dissipated by any diminution in the quality of the services being offered by the private partner; essentially an agency problem in economic terminology.

The nature of this monitoring and regulation, which is often the result of consultation and negotiations between the public and private partners, largely depends on the type of security involved. In regulation theory, if the industry is fairly well established and technologically unprogressive, then cost-based, rate-of-return regulation is the norm, albeit with the danger of the onset of Averch–Johnson effects, that is, overinvestment if the suppliers' capital costs are less than the rate-of-return. In general, with more dynamic sectors, where there is potential for serious technical change, price-capping is generally used to ensure consumers gain from temporal downward shifts in the cost curve. Applying this to transportation security, in cases where manual inspections are the norm the theory would suggest the private suppliers have contracts involving their costs being reimbursed, whereas with electronic scanning of containers where there are ongoing technology advances reducing costs, price-capping contracts, with appropriate quality stipulations, are relevant for a further fostering of technical progress in the equipment.

What do we conclude from this brief discussion? Following the sentiment of Jean-Jacques Laffont and Jean Tirole (1993), public–private partnerships are, as a group, only one form of governance structure that affects the continuum of the level of state regulation of public and privately owned firms. But the PPP group itself is far from homogeneous and has its own internal continuum reflecting the roles of the two sectors. As such, there are circumstances and conditions under which they may provide an optimal structure for providing some elements of security in the transportations supply chain. But equally, there are circumstances when they are inappropriate, and perhaps more often, when contracts are poorly structured.

5.6 OUTSOURCING SECURITY

From the perspective of transportation service providers, there is the option of handling security internally or of outsourcing it. Outsourcing entails a transportation company buying in security services or equipment from specialist outside suppliers rather than providing them itself. The specialized nature of many security activities makes it inefficient for many small companies to have their own security divisions, while economies of scale in security provision, and also possible economies of scope across many types of security services, make it ideal for specialized security firms to serve numerous markets. As Carl Endorf (2004) puts it, 'Most companies are not in the security business. They want to sell their goods and services, not worry about providing security services.' Having said this, there are opportunity costs in outsourcing security.

The general efficiency issues that arise revolve around the degree of outsourcing that is desirable, the criteria that can be used to find them, and the best methods by which the external supplier can be managed.[8] To put it simply, there are dangers in outsources, not least of which lies in the importance of giving potentially sensitive information and responsibilities to outside companies. Basically, a transportation undertaking may outsource full, partial or no responsibility for security, with the decision largely dependent on being able to identify the areas of risk and uncertainty, and the relative costs of outsourcing, including its impact on its own productive activities.

There are also matters of whether integration should be lateral, in terms of buying in for the core component of the supply chain, or whether it should be backward into inputs or forward into later stages of distribution. For example, airlines often outsource their booking (a backward element) and their destination baggage handling (a forward element) as well as subcontracting flights (a lateral element). All have implications for the security of the overall product, which is moving passengers and their belongings. They also add legal layers of complexity regarding responsibility. In the airline case, ultimately security decisions regarding outsourcing will depend both on the legal liability carriers have for protecting their passengers, their baggage, and the general public, and the potential financial costs of civil actions or lost business should their security arrangements fail. While outsourcing may reduce the costs of security, it may not shift the legal liability and, even if it does, it may not shift the public's perception of who is responsible.

NOTES

1. The Public Choice School of economics points to the almost paramount role of government in all economic decision-making; see Dennis Mueller (2003).
2. Although this right is strictly limited; for example individuals in the US cannot have a nuclear weapon as a security measure to protect against an attack by another individual or country.
3. With its assumptions, neoclassical theory cannot differentiate between institutions that are really different, for example between a socialist economy and a private-ownership economy or, say, between a money-using economy and a barter economy.
4. At the extreme it could be argued that the only genuine public goods (that is, those that are both fully non-rival and non-excludable) involve the enforcement of property rights.
5. There are, in fact, few genuine market failures. Paul Samuelson (1954) for example pointed to the problems of public goods, Francis Edgeworth (1881) to the challenges of an empty core, and Stiglitz and Rothschild (1976) to asymmetric information issues.

Most failures associated with markets come from government failures, such as the inadequate allocation of property rights (Coase, 1960) that leads to incomplete contracts and trading.

6. The issue is to demonstrate that state intervention can improve on the status quo. In some cases such actions may worsen the situation – a 'policy intervention failure'. Here I would not completely agree with Oliver Williamson in his Nobel address, where he says that, 'Private sector contracting experienced market failures, by reason of positive transactions costs, but there was no corresponding concept for public sector failures'. This gap is now gradually being filled, at least in transportation policy analysis, by the work of the Organisation for Economic Co-operation and Development (1992), Clifford Winston (2006) and others.
7. Aidan Vining et al. (2005) provide some North American transportation examples, and Guasch et al. (2008) South American examples of the detailed issues that can lead to renegotiations and the various costs involved.
8. These subjects are discussed in the context of supply chain management by Oliver Williamson (2008).

6. Security and air transportation

I don't like getting patted down and taking off my shoes at the airport
Rebecca Miller

6.1 INTRODUCTION

Having spent time on the broader aspects of the economics of transportation security, we now move to a series of chapters that focus on particular issues and specific modes. These are in a way extended case studies that within them have more details of the particular nuances involved in making various aspects of transportation provision and use more secure. Choices of what to include are made in part on the grounds of the importance of the topic, but also reflect the degree of material available and the studies completed on each. We begin with air transportation.

At certain times, particular modes of transportation attract more security attention than their strict importance in the economy in terms of their contributions to National Income would seem to justify. At the end of the twentieth century, and into the twenty-first, air transportation has largely fulfilled this role. Although in countries such as Israel, bus bombs have been widely used, as have car bombs in Iraq, they tend to be more localized in their impacts and seldom pose a major threat to international transportation or huge numbers of people. Kaplan (2009) sums up the situation regarding air transportation rather well:

> You get a lot of victims at once. There is a lot of bang for the buck . . . There is a particular horror attached to transportation attacks because passengers are in effect helpless in a situation like that. . . In addition, the dramatic nature of airliner attacks attracts media attention and can help inspire fear in the populace, two major aims of most terrorist operations.

This is also not actually to imply that aviation is not an important form of transportation. It accounts for about 1 percent of the US and European Union's gross domestic product, it carriers between 35 percent and 40 percent of international trade, according to the basis of the calculation, by value, and is important for the carriage of exotics and high value, low bulk components as well as being vital for tourism in many parts of the world. It is, however, a highly visible means of transportation, is involved in many international markets, and is technologically sophisticated. In many countries air travel epitomizes capitalism and the role of countries like the United States in global politics.

In addition, for a number of reasons it can be a soft target for attack. Technically, although this has been changing, aircraft are physically vulnerable to such things as relatively small bombs and the taking over of a cockpit. There are long periods when aircraft are well away from standard security forces. For these reasons, and also because it is a mass mode of transportation that leads to a concentration of individuals, it has been the subject of numerous attacks.

These attacks on the aviation sector have been on various parts of the air transportation supply chain. The most common have been the 'skyjacking' of aircraft[1] or destruction of aircraft in flight, such as the bringing down of Pan Am Flight 103 over Lockerbie, Scotland, but there have also been attacks on airport terminals (such as that by the Abu Nidal Organization on Rome's Fiumicino and Vienna International Airport in 1985, and by the Japanese Red Army at Lod Airport, Israel in 1972), on runways (for example by the IRA's mortar attack on Heathrow in 1994), and by missiles fired at commercial aircraft (including two anti-aircraft missiles fired at an Israeli airliner taking off near the Kenyan city of Mombasa in 2002).

In numerical terms, between 1948 and 1957, there were 15 skyjackings but this rose to 48 in the following decade. The trend then accelerated, with 38 skyjackings in 1968 and 82 the following year. From 1968 to 1977, there were 414 hijackings, averaging over 40 a year. These were mainly in the US and were often executed by individuals seeking money, 'Andy Warhol's 15 minutes of fame', or to obtain political asylum with the smaller number in Europe being largely by organized terrorist groups with political agendas.

Official reactions to skyjackings and similar activities were initially slow, and especially so in the US, mainly because the airlines were afraid of scaring passengers away, thus limiting the deterrent effects. The major change came about, at least in the US, in November 1972 when Southern Airways Flight 49 was skyjacked and three men armed with guns and hand grenades threatened to crash it into a Tennessee nuclear reactor. Random searches of passengers gave way to searches of all passengers. The watershed in Canada, with much more rigorous screening being introduced in 1985, was the destruction of an Air India flight from Toronto to New Delhi in June, and the death of two baggage handlers in Tokyo after a bomb exploded that was loaded on a flight from Vancouver.

The response in North America was due to changes in the nature of attacks and the motivations underlying them. Skyjackings as we have seen had been taking place for a diversity of reasons. Some have been for pure publicity or the personal gain of the skyjackers, and the terror imparted has been more or less a side-effect of the action. These personal motives vary; they have involved the seeking of financial ransom but more often they have been by individuals and families seeking to leave a particular country to gain asylum elsewhere. In other cases, the attacks have been for direct terror reasons, to either produce material damage or to threaten to do so to obtain political ends. The use of skyjacked civilian aircraft in the attacks on New York and Northern Virginia, together with the thwarted one on Washington, DC in 2001 were largely for symbolic reasons to show the vulnerability of the US major institutions: financial, military and political. Other political actions elsewhere have been aimed at getting the release of prisoners held by the authorities.

Box 6.1 offers a short-listing, together with a few basic details, of some of the major skyjacking and bombing incidents involving aviation since the late 1960s. These do not necessarily reflect the most serious in number of fatalities or any other parameters but rather are selected to indicate the diversity of targets, the variety of groups involved, the number of airlines affected, and the countries that have been involved. It is a diverse picture, and this adds to the problems of ensuring the security of aircraft.

There have been economic arguments advanced, most notably by Cauley and Iksoon Im (1988) and Button (2012a), that some of the changing patterns of acts against air travelers have been the result of anti-terrorist measures as opposed to a neutral shift of objectives by the perpetrators. The attackers have moved to relatively softer targets as security has been tightened in situations where previous attacks had taken place. In particular, looking at the period to 1980 for which they had data, they found that enhanced security, and most notably the introduction of metal detectors in 1973 in the US, led to fewer skyjackings but an increase in other types of terrorist activities related to air travel.

6.2 THE COSTS OF AIRLINE SECURITY

The nature and scale of air transportations security changed considerably after 2001, and did so markedly in the United States (Seidenstat, 2004). This has been accompanied by increases in the costs of security, and in the relative burden of the costs on stakeholders.

There are a variety of costs associated with securing air transportation, and with most other modes some of these are much more transparent than others.[2] Table 6.1, for example, provides a comparison of the recorded costs directly borne by airline travelers for security measures, but these are often only partial in the sense that airlines themselves have higher costs of

BOX 6.1 THE DIVERSE NATURE OF SKYJACKINGS

- 1968: Members of Popular Front for the Liberation of Palestine hijacked an El Al flight from Rome to Tel Aviv. Hijackers and the hostages went free.
- 1976: Palestinian hijack of an Air France flight ending at Entebbe Airport, Uganda. Israeli commandos killed hijackers and rescued 105 people; 3 passengers and a commando killed.
- 1977: Lufthansa flight hijacked by Palestinians on flight from Palma de Mallorca to Frankfurt. In Mogadishu commandos killed the 3 hijackers, freed 86 hostages, but pilot died.
- 1985: Members of the Abu Nidal Organization hijacked a flight from Athens to Cairo and flew it to Malta where 60 people died when Egyptian commandos stormed the aircraft.
- 1986: Twenty-two people died when Pakistani security forces stormed a plane at Karachi, carrying 400 passengers and crew.
- 1986: Sixty-three people were killed when an Iraqi Airways flight crashed near Arar, Saudi Arabia after being hijacked.
- 1988: Family hijacked a flight from Irkutsk to Leningrad to escape from the USSR. In storming the plane a stewardess and 3 passengers died and the mother was killed by a son, with 4 committing suicide.
- 1994: FedEx Flight 705 hijacked by a disgruntled employee to attack the FedEx HQ. He was subdued by the crew.
- 1994: Air France Flight 8969 was hijacked from Algiers by GIA terrorists planning to crash it into the Eiffel Tower. After killing 3 passengers, GIGN commandos stormed the plane in Marseilles, killing hijackers and freeing all passengers.
- 1996: Ethiopian Airlines plane crashed into the Indian Ocean in the Comoros Islands after hijackers refused to allow the pilot to land and refuel it, killing 125 passengers.
- 2000: Philippine Airlines flight was hijacked en route from Davao, Philippines to Manila. The hijacker parachuted from the aircraft; his body was later found.
- 2001: Nineteen terrorists hijacked American and United Airlines flights. Two planes were crashed into New York City's World Trade Center killing 2998 people and one into the Pentagon, killing over 100. An attack on the US Capitol Building in Washington, DC was averted when passengers intervened and crashed the plane, killing all.
- 2007: An Aeroflot Airbus A320 flying from Moscow to Geneva was hijacked by a drunk man in Prague; crew and passengers were released after he was arrested.
- 2011: A Turkish Airline flight from Oslo to Istanbul hijacked in Bulgarian airspace by a man claiming to have a bomb he would detonate unless the plane returned to Norway. Passengers overpowered him and the flight safely landed at Atatürk Airport.
- 2012: An attempt was made to hijack a Tianjin Airlines flight from Hotan to Ürümqi by Uyghur hijackers. Six off-duty police officers overcame the hijackers.

- 2014: Attempted hijacking of a Pegasus Airlines plane flying from Kharki to Istanbul. The pilots turned off the inflight monitors, landing at Istanbul's Sabiha Gökçen Airport rather than Sochi as demanded. The man was detained and taken to the Istanbul Security Headquarters.
- 2014: An Ethiopian Airlines flight between Addis Ababa and Rome was forced to proceed to Geneva by the co-pilot seeking asylum in Switzerland. On landing, the hijacker was arrested.

Table 6.1 *Average security charges per traveler at airports (2002)*

Country	Average charge per passenger
Canada	$14.50
Germany	$10.57
Israel	$8.03
France	$6.88
Australia	$5.19
United States	$5.00
Netherlands	$4.13
Russia	$2.04
Italy	$1.90
United Kingdom	$0.00

Source: Waters and Yu (2003).

additional training of staff, the fitting of secure cabin devices, and, especially in Israel and the US, the requirement to carry air marshals that take up otherwise revenue-earning seats. These are, at least, partly subsumed in fares rather than explicit security fees or taxes. The same holds for some airport security. The zero passenger fee for the UK seen in Table 6.1, for example, is because its airports must meet national and international security standards and the costs of doing so are passed on through the general fees charged to airlines and land-side concessionaires.

Airport Security in the US

Before the 11 September 2001 terrorist attacks, US airlines were responsible for providing passenger screening and the Federal Aviation Administration was supposed to promulgate performance and training standards. The airlines hired roughly 19 500 screeners from private security companies to perform screening procedures at US airports (US Government

Accountability Office, 2005). After the 2001 attacks, some observers have claimed that reliance on private screeners was disastrous, but it should be noted that the screeners were subject to government regulations. In any case, the Transportation Security Administration (TSA) was created, and in February 2002 it assumed responsibility for screening at virtually all US airports. By the end of 2002 the TSA deployed a workforce that, accounting for temporary employees, had grown to more than 50 000 screeners.

Passengers from 2014 paid $5.60 for each leg of their flight, up to a maximum of $11.20 per round trip, to help pay for security screening. Airlines then remit the fees to the TSA to support its annual budget of roughly $5.5 billion. To facilitate flexibility in staffing that can respond to changes in airline service, airports have been given the option to replace federal screeners with screeners from private companies. But private screeners are still overseen by federal employees and are required to be paid at least as much as federal ones and to have undergone the same training. Not surprisingly, with such conditions only a handful of small airports have applied to the government to use privately employed screeners.

In response to air travelers' complaints about the excessive delays created by TSA screening at major airports, a 'registered traveler' program was initiated to create special, speedier airport security lines for people who are willing to pay an annual fee of $50 to $100 and undergo background checks. However, the TSA refused to follow Congress's direction to conduct background checks on registered traveler applicants and to provide expedited screening to those who passed. That undercut the potential value that the three approved registered traveler companies offered to members, and appears to have caused the largest provider to enter bankruptcy in June 2009. Airlines, such as American and United, tried to expedite screening at certain airports by instituting special security lines for travelers who are elite members of their frequent flier programs.

In October 2011, the TSA initiated a Precheck program that allowed selected US citizens and resident alien members of the American, Delta, United, Alaska, Hawaiian, Virgin America, Southwest, Air Canada, JetBlue, and Sun Country frequent flyer programs, members of Global Entry, NEXUS, SENTRI and active duty members of the US military to receive expedited screening for domestic and select international itineraries. By August 2015, this program was available at 156 airports. To obtain a known traveler number, eligible persons paid a $85 fee, were interviewed and finger-printed.

In addition to the screening and other on-ground security measures initiated or extended after September 2001, on-plane security was tightened with the hardening of cockpit doors (the Installed Physical Secondary Barriers program) to prevent non-consensual entry, the Federal Flight

Deck Officer program (giving training to flight-deck crew to carry and use firearms), and a major extension of the Federal Air Marshal Service were funded. These security measures cost the US government and the airlines nearly $1 billion per annum. Stewart and Mueller (2008) provide a critique of the value for money of these measures, something I return to later.

Performance of Airport Security

An efficient airport security system allocates resources based on cost–benefit considerations by directing expenditures towards detecting and preventing the greatest threats to safety from materializing. Although I am not aware of a formal economic assessment of the TSA's passenger screening, the Department of Homeland Security, the Government Accountability Office and TSA routinely test screeners' ability to intercept weapons smuggled through checkpoints. The results have been poor. Both the US Government Accountability Office and Homeland Security found that screening was no more effective by April 2005 than before 11 September, and in 2006 screeners failed 20 of TSA's 22 tests (Akers, 2007). The US Government Accountability Office (2008) reported that covert tests through June 2007 conducted by the TSA's Office of Inspection identified vulnerabilities in the commercial aviation system at airports of all sizes. But the TSA apparently lacks a systematic process to ensure that the Office of Inspection's recommendations are appropriately incorporated to improve airport security.

Current screening procedures are also not fully efficient. The annual cost of TSA security includes its budget of $5.5 billion, several billions of dollars in time costs incurred by passengers waiting to be screened, and $1.1 billion in lost revenue to airlines from reduced passenger volume at major airports (Blalock et al., 2007). The Office of Inspection reports in 2009 that TSA has spent more than $800 million on new air passenger screening technology during 2002 to 2008, but has not used any of it by that time.

It is, of course, difficult to assess the benefits of TSA screening because we do not know of any terrorist attacks that screening has prevented, only cases where there were violations of laws regarding what could be carried on a plane. In any case, federal screeners intercepted some 7 million prohibited items by 2005, but only 600 were firearms while the rest were nail scissors, penknives and the like (Applebaum, 2005). Those findings are consistent with many critics' assessment of TSA's first-generation passenger and bag screening: it could stop most amateurs but it seems unlikely to be a deterrent to anyone seriously committed to bringing weapons or some type of explosive onto a plane.[3] Instead of expending billions of dollars in time and money to confiscate firearms, almost all of which were probably intended for recreational use, and using Federal Air Marshals, Stewart and Mueller (2008) conclude that it was far more cost effective to put bulletproof doors on cockpits, which the airline industry did for some $300 million to $500 million; a range dependent on the estimated cost of having planes out of service during the fitting.

Other inefficiencies suggest that airports could obtain the current level of security at much lower cost. In economic terms there appears to be X-inefficiency in the system. For example, the TSA stipulates which contractor may be used for screening when the job is outsourced rather than leaving this to the airport that is likely more familiar with local needs and suppliers (Ybarra, 2013). Another example are the large costs associated with passengers' excessive waiting times at heavily used airports that could have been sharply reduced if the TSA had more rapidly implemented its nationwide registered traveler program with technology that expedited screening.

Wait times would also be reduced if the TSA's labor force were flexible and could be deployed in response to the peaking characteristics of air travel throughout the day and during certain times of year. The TSA's large budget has come under fire for wasteful expenditures on inappropriate or outdated technology and a bloated labor force described by critics as 'Thousands Standing Around'. The TSA was embarrassed when a graduate student exposed the uselessness of its boarding-pass identification check by developing a fake boarding pass that would enable an individual to pass through security and get to any airport gate. In the summer of 2008, a traveler wearing an Osama bin Laden T-shirt under his coat cleared security at Minneapolis airport with a phony Northwest Airlines boarding pass and no photo identification. As a consequence of all this, Stross (2006) argues that conducting basic investigation and intelligence appears to be more cost effective than performing identification checks, maintaining secret databases, and instituting no-fly lists, although he does not provide any rigorous analysis.

A more fundamental concern is whether the TSA should even exist. One alternative that is likely to be superior to the TSA on cost–benefit grounds is a variant of Israel's model, where a branch of law enforcement receives additional funding and is responsible for questioning and identifying suspicious passengers. Turning to the private sector, security firms have long been able to provide effective and subtle security for millions of customers at high-risk facilities in the US, such as casinos in Las Vegas and Atlantic City and major amusement parks. Private security firms could be hired at airports, not just to replace federal screeners with private screeners, but also to develop security strategies and make safety investments to anticipate and respond to potential terrorist attacks without being constrained by the federal government's regulatory oversight. Such firms could also be bonded, giving them strong financial incentives to provide effective security. As noted earlier, the government successfully regulated the 19 500 private screeners hired by airlines prior to 11 September 2001. Indeed, it has been claimed that greater government bureaucracy since then has discouraged research and development of new innovative solutions to combat terrorism, causing a political disagreement over whether the government or the private sector should drive the development of security technology (Luzadder, 2006).

6.3 THE FUNDING OF TRANSPORTATION SECURITY

Security is costly. Part of the burden is borne indirectly by transportation users who have their movements interrupted and are obliged to bear additional administrative costs and oversight. As we have seen in Table 6.1, there are many cases where there are specific security charges imposed on the air transportation system and the revenues hypothecated to state security expenditures. In others, there are, as we have also seen, systems like that in the UK whereby regulations are set and their costs then passed to air transportation users as a general cost through airport charges. This potpourri of approaches is largely determined by expediency and influenced by notions of equity, and in many case initiated, at least at first, as a short-term need to meet a sudden requirement for enhanced security.

As we can see from Figure 6.1 relating to the United States, however, the total sums involved with specific fees can be large and often rise over time. In aggregate, however, they seldom cover the full costs of aviation security. In the US case, cost has fluctuated between somewhat over 20 percent to just over 30 percent since 2002; in 2014, for example, it was about 32 percent.

The public sector contribution to aviation security varies between countries, as well as within individual countries over time. This may be seen as reflecting national needs and priorities in terms of perceived threats, as well as variations in the costs of national resources and the underlying institutional structures involved. Regarding the former, after the events of 11 September 2001, there was an initial concern with screening to prevent weapons being taken aboard aircraft, but after the attempt to blow up planes traveling between the UK and Canada and the US using peroxide-based liquid explosives in 2006, different limitations were placed on what could be taken as carry-on baggage. This in turn led to a greater

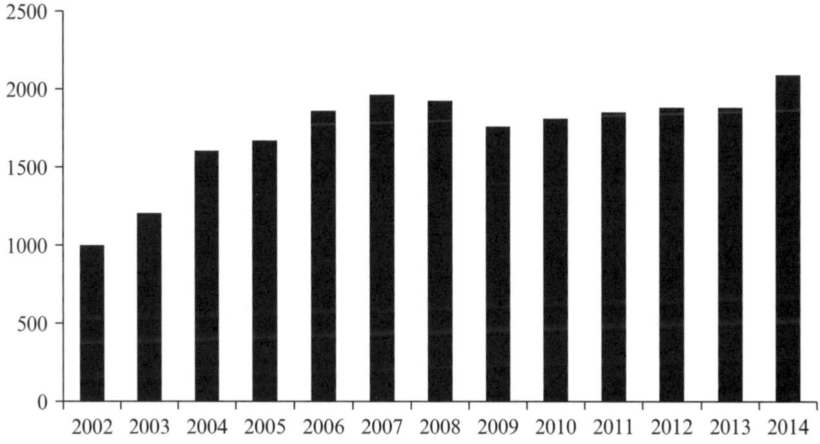

Source: http://www.tsa.gov/stakeholders/historical-fee-collection-data.

Figure 6.1 US aviation security fees collected ($ million)

emphasis on securing checked bags that, in the United States, increased by 30 percent.

Regarding budgeting for greater security, the US initiated a major upgrading and reorientation of its aviation security after 2001, with significant initial capital outlays on equipment, manpower training and institutional developments, followed by somewhat varying annual expenditures influenced by opinions on the dangers involved and the best ways of combating them (Oster and Strong, 2008). What is clear from the US picture, and probably the case in most countries, is that the perceptions of what is needed as expressed by those responsible for implementing security measures (the TSA in the US case) often differ from the views of those with overall control of the security budget (basically Congress in the US), or those potentially immediately concerned with its impacts.

Where there is some flexibility to more closely align these views is in the use of offsetting passenger security and air carrier security fees of the type initiated in the US in 2002 and discussed in a different context in section 6.2. These fees were aimed at their outset at reducing the burden on general taxpayers for financing these activities, transferring part of the burden to identifiable user groups who benefit from security beyond what is normally provided to the public, and to make the system more transparent to a third group of stakeholders, the general population. These fees broadly

Table 6.2 TSA annual appropriations and security fee incomes ($ millions)

Year	2002	2003	2004	2005	2006	2007	2008	2009	2010	2011
TSA appropriation	4340	7662	4775	5516	5876	6403	6180	7630	7321	7231
Passenger security fees	995	1200	1600	1616	1660	1710	1420	1506	1558	1598
Air carrier security fees	133	253	283	307	350	573	412	407	282	400

Source: Adapted from: http://www.gao.gov/modules/ereport/handler.php?1=1&path=/ereport/GAO-12-342SP/data_center_savings/Homeland_security_Law_enforcement/48._Passenger_Aviation_Security_Fees.

follow the guidance issued by the ICAO regarding cost recovery for airport charges, including fees related to aviation security, and the extent to which fees should offset security costs. From an economic perspective, while they move the system nearer to a market-based approach, their aim is cost recovery in a more equity fashion and function neither as an allocative mechanism nor as an indicator of where security funds could optimally be directed.

Along these lines, Oster and Strong (2008) found, regarding the methods of funding US aviation security, that while the TSA's request for $1600 million of funding for aviation security in 2001 was met completely by congressional appropriations, and over-funding continued until 2005 (for example, in 2004, the request for $3617 million was over-funded by $107 million), after this appropriations fell short of TSA requests (for example, the TSA request for 2007 amounted to $3889 million, but appropriations were only for $1990 million). Additional revenues have come from the offsetting fees levied on airlines and passengers, with the TSA from 2002 through to 2011 collecting about $18 billion in fees, compared to approximately $63 billion appropriated for aviation security activities over the period. In other words about 29 percent of appropriations for aviation were for security-related activities during this time frame (Table 6.2).

6.4 ECONOMIC ASSESSMENT OF THE ATTACKS OF 11 SEPTEMBER 2001

Given the scale and the consequences of the attacks on the New York World Trade Center, the Pentagon and the White House or Capital

Building and their wide-ranging implications, we divert to consider the economic aspects of the events. In particular, the scale of the economic repercussions of the attack extended well beyond the immediate areas and the airlines, and had extensive implications in terms of how security is handled.

The attack itself, or at least its form, was unexpected. The New York World Trade Center had been threatened before with a truck bomb attack in 1993, but there seems to have been no intelligence concerning a possible air-based attack. The populations of New York and Northern Virginia, and the airlines and their passengers felt the shorter-term economic implications of 11 September. Large parts of the US economy, for example, were hit by the closure of the air traffic system for a number of days. In numerical terms, on 10 September 2001 US airports handled 38 047 commercial flights, on 12 September they handled 252, and one week later (18 September) there were 34 743 flights. The most direct visible economic impacts on transportation were inevitably on the airlines and their support industries such as air traffic control and airports. The aviation sector had been growing steadily prior to 2001, with traffic volumes rising by an average rate of 3.6 percent between 1990 and 2000, although there were indications of a slow-down in line with trends in the US economy from the first quarter of 2001, patterns consistent with a number of other markets around the globe. The effects of the events of 11 September 2001 were to reduce demand for air travel due to both the direct effects of potential passengers being fearful of flying and the additional costs of air travel as security measures were significantly stepped up. US air travel fell by 20 percent between September and December 2001 (Figure 6.2). Added to this, the global economy went into a recession, partly tied to the fears of political instability the attacks had engendered, and partly reflecting the continuation of the downturn that had begun in 2001 as part of the short-term Juglar business cycle.

Estimating the specific costs to the airlines of the 2001 attacks is not easy given the macroeconomic downturn that was already in progress.[4] Blunk et al. (2006) seek to separate the effects by establishing a counterfactual simulating the likely trends in air travel if there had been no attack and no significant stepping up of security, but allowing for the changing macroeconomic conditions of the early 2000s. They find that following a near 55 percent reduction in revenue passenger-miles in September 2001, the ultra short-term effect, the short-term impact up to December 2002, while fluctuating by the month, was about 12 percent. In a similar exercise, Harumi Ito and Darin Lee (2005) calculated a negative transitory shock of over 30 percent on the US demand for air travel, and an ongoing negative shock continuing to at least 2003 amounting to roughly 7.4 percent that

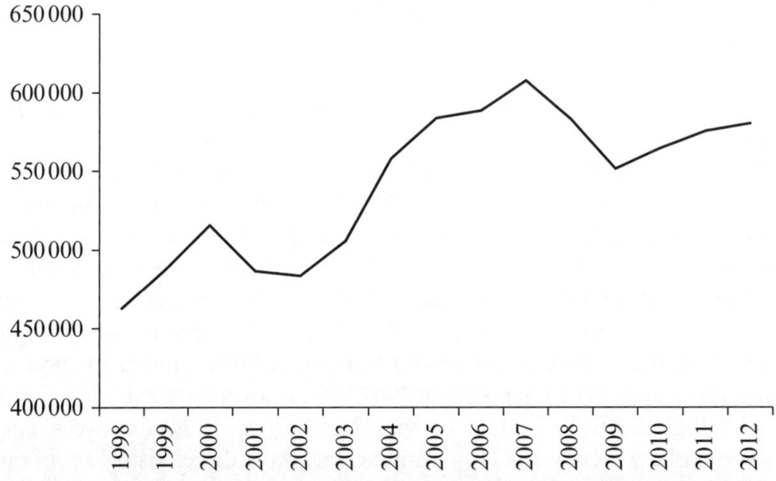

Figure 6.2 United States domestic air passenger-miles (1998–2012 in thousands)

cannot be explained by such things as macroeconomics cycles. According to Peter Gordon et al.'s (2009) assessment, however, this may be an underestimate because of disproportionate costs of initiating security at the largest US airports.

Assuming that security measures, once implemented, would restore confidence in the airline industry, taking a somewhat narrower, longer-term view, Blalock et al. (2007) focus on the implications of the higher security costs of air travel post-11 September. Looking at baggage screening measures they found that originating passengers were reduced by about 6 percent at all airports and by 9 percent at the 50 largest US airports. The number of originating passengers was treated as the key variable, because those transferring at an airport did not have their bags re-screened or their identifications rechecked, these actions were not affected by the new measures. Further, as may be expected, shorter flights were more affected because the screening is a fixed cost of a trip and thus weighs more in the overall cost of a flight. Seeking to put a monetary value on this, the authors estimate airlines lost about $1.2 billion in revenue due to this demand effect.

Blalock et al. (2007), along with similar work by Rossiter and Dresner (2004) and Waters and Yu (2003), extend their analysis to consider social costs of 11 September, and in particular those of the modal diversion to automobiles for shorter journeys as the generalized costs of airport security and concerns over safety affect the relative attractiveness of air travel. While their findings differ in detail because of diverse assumptions concerning, amongst other things, the cross-elasticity of demand between air and car travel, all found substantial social costs, albeit with large standard deviations, in terms of additional road fatalities. Blalock et al., for example, come up with an estimate of about an additional 100 road deaths in the US as an immediate aftermath of the attacks, while Rossiter and Dresner estimated the figure as up to 66.2 extra deaths per annum.[5]

While it is difficult to assess the costs of security measures, evaluating the benefits of greater aviation security are, as we have repeatedly emphasized in previous chapters, even more challenging. Here we focus narrowly and directly on some of the work done following the 11 September attacks. Again, however, it is clear that the breadth of the benefits were wider than just those affecting the US, for example the security measures initiated in aviation by the United States' authorities clearly have resulted in greater longer-term security across the international aviation network.

Within their cost–benefit framework focusing exclusively on on-plane security initiatives, Stewart and Mueller (2008) use prior experiences of attacks on airlines to assess the net social worth of the US security initiative, finding, for example, that the Air Marshal Services costs $180 million for every life saved, while hardened cockpit doors only cost $800 per life.

The problem here is both in working out the technical efficiency of the policies in preventing a successful terrorist attack, or at least containing its adverse effects, and in putting a value on this efficiency. Stewart and Mueller make use of what are often called standard values of life that are deployed in areas such as road safety where incidents are much more common. The problem is that the numbers used are quite wide ranging depending on the methodology used in their calculation and the nature of their ultimate application. To estimate the reduction in risk associated with an on-plane security measure, use is made of historic data. The inevitable problem here, as highlighted earlier, is that the number of incidents is small and they are diverse in nature, and that perpetrators are responsive to countermeasures and adjust their strategies accordingly.

6.5 ICAO AND SECURITY

International coordination of air transportation security is relatively new. With the benefit of hindsight, it may seem hard to imagine how the need to address acts of sabotage, unlawful seizure of aircraft and the use of civil aircraft in terrorist attacks could have been overlooked by the drafters of the Convention on International Civil Aviation (the Chicago Convention), which in 1944, under the auspices of the UN, laid the modern institutional framework for international air transportation. This laid out the various 'freedom of the skies' that has allowed for the development of international agreements on airline traffic and established the International Civil Aviation Organization (ICAO), which allowed for their further development. Security was not, however, a major interest at the Convention and the focus was on establishing air services.

When security did arise as a serious issue in the late 1960s, the Chicago Convention was adapted to provide an international framework for addressing acts of unlawful interference. Since that time the ICAO has modified and updated its institutional oversight over security 11 times. In addition, individual countries, or groups of countries, have initiated their own security policies and measures that have often extended beyond the ICAO's regulations and have also been active in enforcing international air transportation policies.

The major problem with reaching international agreement on terrorism is that much of the damage caused by attacks is geographically focused but the perpetrators can be widely spread. In economic terms, there are significant beneficial externalities for any country engaging in trade in airline services in having a secure system, but these benefits extend to the origins and destinations of flight from and to that country that are external to it. There is thus an incentive for a country to be a free-rider, enjoying considerable benefits from airline service trading partners that have security in place but not extending its own security beyond that meeting its own needs. Added to this, aircraft are extremely mobile assets and their use often transcends national markets. In this context there are economies of standardization in having common security hardware and software on planes.

Before 11 September perhaps the most significant attack on an international flight, excluding skyjackings, was the bombing of Pan Am Flight 103 over Lockerbie, Scotland in 1988, when 270 people died. This led to tighter security regarding checking passengers and their baggage. But the scale and the nature of the attack differed from those of 2001, and in particular the Pan Am plane had not in itself been used as a weapon. Whilst this has stimulated greater international coordination of security policies on both a bilateral and a multilateral basis regarding baggage control and inspections, as seen by the bombing of the Russian Metrojet flight between Sharm el-Sheikh International Airport in Egypt and Pulkovo Airport, Saint Petersburg in October 2015, satisfactory enforcement is still often lacking.

Initially, the early ICAO security-related work had focused on developing

Standards and Recommended Practices (SARPs) for inclusion in Annex 17 of the Chicago Convention. This sets minimum safety standards that Member States are expected to meet, for example to have a civil aviation security organization and a documented security program.

Over the years, the ICAO's work in the field of aviation security has broadened and is now carried out in three interrelated areas:

- Policy initiatives. These are focused primarily on maintaining the currency of Annex 17. Security policy is the responsibility of the Aviation Security and Facilitation Policy Section, which promotes the implementation of Annex 17 through seminars and workshops for personnel from airports, airlines and law enforcement agencies, as well as through the dissemination of guidance material.
- Audits focusing on the capability of contracting states to oversee their aviation security activities. These are performed under the Universal Security Audit Program.
- Assistance to states that are unable to address serious security deficiencies highlighted by audits. The Implementation Support and Development Program facilitates short-term or urgent security-related assistance to states with longer-term project assistance available from the ICAO's Technical Co-operation Bureau.

Since the late 1980s, the ICAO has relied on the advice of 27 state nominated and five industrial observer members who sit on its Aviation Security Panel. In addition, other bodies of experts that play a pivotal role in the ICAO's security work are the Ad Hoc Group of Specialists on the Detection of Explosives and the International Explosives Technical Commission. These specialists focus on updating the Technical Annex to the *Convention on the Marking of Plastic Explosives for the Purpose of Detection*, which came into force in 1998. Each state party to the Convention is required to prohibit and prevent the manufacture in its territory of unmarked plastic explosives.

The organization's other activities in the field of aviation security include efforts to enhance the security of travel documents, notably the Machine Readable Travel Document Program, and improve the training of security personnel. In addition it provides support for regional security initiatives.

While the efforts of the UN's body have clearly been important for enhancing international aviation security, its role, as can be seen from our short history, has often been reactive rather than proactive, and frequently devoid of any real economic analysis. In some cases, countries such as the US and multinational entities such as the EU have acted beyond the organization's basic requirements and have used unilateral monitoring and policing powers.

One problem with the ICAO is that it was never designed to deal with security matters; it was formed essentially to facilitate trade in international air services. As such its expertise and approach is often legalistic and aimed at institutional design rather than at addressing the more detailed matters of security. It is also a large, and thus cumbersome, body that requires coalitions of interests to move policy. National differences in concerns about security and the costs of implementing measures make formations of such coalitions challenging. Additionally, individual states have their own particular terrorist threats and this often requires specific reciprocity between pairs or small groups of countries rather than more generic measures.

6.6 CONCLUDING THOUGHTS

The security of the air transportation system has largely dominated public consciousness regarding transportation security in the United States, and especially so since the events of 2001. It is a highly visible mode of transportation and has been subjected to a diverse range of attacks. The economic costs of these attacks, although at the personal level often devastating, have not, with the exception of that of 2001, been large in terms of consequences for the US GDP. The challenge for economists is to develop a cost–benefit framework that guides policy-makers into decisions that maximize social welfare in a field where short-term impacts often overshadow the longer-term implications of an attack, or the probability of an attack being repeated.

While, as we have seen, there are ways of dealing with these challenges, they tend to be partial in their coverage and more useful for smaller-scale incidents. Regarding large-scale security breaches, the macro-implications, such as those associated with the 2001 attacks in the US, really come within the purview of general equilibrium analysis, an area where, despite the possible use of input–output analysis or computable general equilibrium models, economists are still developing good empirical methodologies.

The challenge, as with many other areas of security policy, lies in the fact that terrorist attacks are not easily amenable to standard actuarial analysis: again a matter of uncertainty. While there are, albeit rather limited, ways of gleaning information of the potential and nature of attacks on the aviation sector using intelligence and subjective assessments, these are very much second or third best. Added to this are the social costs of adopting some of these methods. These often involve looking at the threat posed by types of individual and not by their access to threatening hardware. This, for example, involves emphasis on the detailed screening of passengers rather than what individuals are carrying or wearing, for example the profiling that is used by Israel. The issue here is one of social cost, and in particular of personal privacy. It is basically a risk-based approach that essentially involves the categorization of individuals by socioeconomic features, and this is not acceptable in all societies. The political arithmetic in the US, for example, makes it unacceptable. From a narrower economic perspective, however, it may well pass a conventional style cost–benefit analysis quite easily.

NOTES

1. Skyjackings are not new; the first recorded was in 1931 in Peru when Byron Rickards, flying a Ford Tri-Motor, was approached on the ground by revolutionaries. He refused to fly them anywhere and after 10 days was informed that the revolution was successful and he could go in return for giving one group member a lift to Lima.
2. In the context of the European Union this is particularly so with the EC Regulation No. 300/2008 allowing any mix of revenue source from the state, airlines, airports, passengers and shippers.
3. The TSA noted that covert testing has led to the development of new technologies, such as body-scanning equipment and two-dimensional X-ray systems at passenger check-points. Body-scanning technologies are more effective than metal detectors at spotting potentially dangerous objects and substances and can do so with minimal radiation exposure, but administration has been slow to introduce those technologies.
4. In addition, the 2001 Air Transportation Safety and Stabilization Act provided $5 billion in short-term support for the industry to partly offset the financial impact of the attack.
5. This provides some support for Mueller's (2004) argument that the unintended consequences of reactions to terrorism can be one of the major costs.

7. The economics of shopping mall security

> Security is the mother of danger and the grandmother of destruction
> Thomas Fuller

7.1 INTRODUCTION

Various elements of transportation networks have historically found themselves prone to attack both in conventional wars and by terrorists, broadly defined. While the focus of these attacks has in the past often involved links and terminals in inter-urban networks – airlines/ airports; railway lines/ railway stations and so on – the local, urban and suburban elements of logistics chains have not been left unscathed. The focus here is on the vulnerability of shopping malls – important urban and suburban interfaces between inbound flows of goods to retail outlets and outbound flows from retail outlets to final consumption. They are an integral part of the modern supply chain, and also an element that has a high profile, and that is difficult to secure (Helferich and Cook, 2002).[1]

Shopping malls provide important retail outlets that offer shoppers economies of scale and scope in their purchasing, and economies of market presence for retailers in their selling. They have grown significantly in number in the US and in many other countries over recent years, with increases in their size and range of facilities provided. They also often act as major recreation centers containing cinemas, bars and food outlets in addition to stores selling commodities to take away. Strolling and hanging-out in malls can also provide a distraction for teenagers, and a place to gain information that helps decision-making when online shopping. Overall, from a security perspective, they represent large gatherings of citizens that offer possible targets for terrorists. Indeed, the US Department of Homeland Security (DHS) categorizes shopping centers, along with other easily accessible public places, as soft targets.

Security has always been an issue at malls but there have been important changes in emphasis (Van Drake, 2001). Traditional security has been focused on preventing petty crimes of theft, minor material damage to the fabric of buildings, and assaults on individuals – collectively called crimes hereafter for brevity (Romano, 1994).[2] These problems continue. For example, in a 1995 survey for the National Retail Federation, the University of Florida found that the average discount store in 1994 had 0.09 physical crimes against customers, ranging from simple assault to rape and murder. That translates into a rate of about 20 crimes against customers per year for chains the size of Wal-Mart and Kmart. This seems to have been taken as an acceptable level of crimes on persons, at least until the end of the twentieth century in the US, with James Overstreet and Richard Clodfelter (1995) finding that 92 percent of a survey of shoppers in malls in Washington, DC, Virginia, North Carolina and Georgia feeling they were safe places to shop. Where there were concerns were in terms of conventional criminal activities involving property, mainly theft in various forms.

This traditional problem of criminality is now overlapped by concerns about the possibility of terrorist attacks.[3] Globally, malls have not been immune from attacks in the past – there have been well over 60 terrorist or terrorist inspired attacks of various size and form at shopping malls since 1998 (LaTourrette et al., 2006) in 21 countries including the UK, Turkey, Israel, Russia and Spain. Many of the attacks have been relatively small-scale and caused few casualties, but the shooting and grenade attack on 21 September 2013 by the al-Shabaab group on the upmarket Westgate shopping mall in Nairobi, Kenya left at least 67 people dead and more than 175 wounded.

The problem is certainly an ongoing one. At the time of writing (11 January 2016) it has just been reported that at least 18 people were killed and 40 others injured when insurgents attacked a shopping mall in Baghdad, Iraq with hand grenades and at least two nearby bombs. As in this case, the majority of these attacks have involved explosives of various types, but there have also been incidents involving firearms and chemicals.

The events of September 2001 have heightened concerns in the US and elsewhere that shopping malls may more frequently become explicit targets for major attack.[4] There have already been numerous actual and thwarted terrorist attacks at US malls, although compared to some attacks overseas, these have been on a relatively minor scale. Five people were killed and four injured in a shooting at a Salt Lake City mall in 2007 by a Bosnian, for example, and in the same year, a 19-year-old man killed nine people, including himself, and injured four others at the Westroads Mall in Omaha, while in 2012, a 22-year-old killed two people in the Clackamas Town Center in Oregon using a semiautomatic rifle before committing suicide. There have also been abortive attempts at terrorism. In November 2007, Nuradin Abdi, a Somali living in Ohio, pleaded guilty to planning, with other al-Qaeda operatives, to blow up a Columbus area shopping mall.

Nevertheless, and for a variety of economic, political and social reasons, the media attention paid to shopping mall security in the US has been much less than to many other parts of the transportation supply chain such as airports, airlines, and chemical and oil movements. Besides any consideration of the costs and difficulties of attacking malls, like other nodes in the transportation system, shopping malls cannot be used as weapons in the same way that aircraft, trucks and other mobile plant can. There is no mobile threat and this, in one sense, changes the ways terrorists may view them (Button et al., 2003).

One of the problems is that the retail industry has treaded warily when discussing terrorist threats for commercial reasons; their implicit cost–benefit calculations do not support making their security measures widely known. Customers expect shopping centers to be free and open, and mall owners and operators have been reluctant to introduce stringent security measures, or at least openly show them as airports have done, that might limit shoppers' access, or scare them off altogether. There is an equal reluctance in many countries to have large-scale electronic surveillance for fear of deterring customers. The UK is something of an outlier in this respect with an estimated 500 000 closed-circuit television cameras in Greater London in 2011 and 4 200 000 in the UK as a whole although only some of these were in shopping malls.

It is also often difficult and expensive for mall operators to have extensive security systems because of the diversity of access points to a mall; in contrast, airports can channel passengers, freight and employees through a limited number of checkpoints. Shoppers are also more sensitive about seeing large numbers of security staff; it affects the 'shopping experience'. Though security officers are usually in uniform, they are not intended to appear threatening and frequently serve a variety of roles as well as security.[5]

There thus seems to be no appetite, at least in North America and most of Western Europe, for making shopping malls closed environments whereby entry is through one point with a metal detector and X-ray, and manned by heavily armed security personnel. The period after the November 2015 attacks in Paris may, however, have shifted that view a little.

7.2 THE ECONOMICS OF SHOPPING MALLS

While the public authorities and the media have regularly expressed concern about the vulnerability of shopping malls to terrorist attack, some 87 percent of US shoppers according to a survey done in March 2005 by the International Council of Shopping Centers (ICSC), a trade association, said they considered enclosed malls to be safe, and shoppers in general seem to make no change to their shopping habits when the government announces an elevated threat of terrorism. This lack of outward public concern is seen in part as a reflection of the lack of major attacks on malls, but also the fact that shopping centers are such an integral part of everyday life that attacks are simply impossible to imagine.

Shopping malls have developed largely due to a combination of new consumer, new products, and new supply-side-chain management philosophies. They are purpose-built logistics centers that allow bulk deliveries of goods to be split at a highly micro level and distributed largely by the private motorcar to points of final consumption, generally the home. Economic synergies also mean that they also often act as nodes in the provision of a variety of services such as banking and dining. There are powerful forces of agglomeration, basically economies of scale, scope and density that foster a concentration of diverse retailers, including the more efficient use of land for what is essentially a consolidation activity. Shopping centers are thus major elements in the modern logistics value chain. Figure 7.1 (after Michael Porter, 1985) outlines the major elements in the value chain. Shopping malls, in their various forms, are part of both outbound logistics and marketing and sales. They take commodities from suppliers and package them, through retail services, to be transported to points of final consumption. In performing this function, the scale of activities involved is considerable.

Numerically, there are over 46 000 shopping centers in the United States, of which about 95 percent are strip malls with retail outlets spread linearly along a street. They employ nearly 11 million people and generated in 2001 over $50 billion in local sales taxation revenue. Each month in 2001 saw nearly 200 million shoppers visiting these centers to undertake some

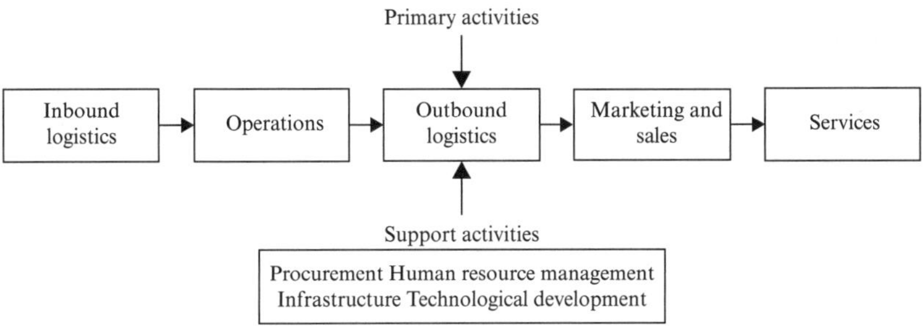

Figure 7.1 The value chain

\$1.8 trillion worth of business – half of all non-automotive sales in the US. They are now so widespread in the US that there are arguments that excess capacity has developed. Other countries have also experienced growth in malls. Australia, for example, has 1360 shopping centers, with the largest attracting over 18 million shoppers a year, and some 2.5 billion in total. They generate well over US\$41 billion in retail sales each year, employ some 500 000 workers, and have an asset value of over US\$50 billion. In the developing countries, shopping malls provide 7 percent of retail revenue in India, 10 percent in Vietnam, 25 percent in China, 28 percent in Indonesia, 39 percent in the Philippines, and 45 percent in Thailand. These countries also contain some of the largest malls. In 2013 the largest fully occupied mall was the Golden Resources Mall in Beijing, China, with a gross leasable floor area of 557 419 m^2; The King of Prussia Mall in Pennsylvania, with 259 500 m^2 of retail space is the largest mall in the US, and 27th largest in the world.

Shopping malls are not homogeneous in their functions and locations, and their various types pose potentially different challenges from the security perspective. They differ by the size of market they serve, the composition of shops that they embrace and the locations in which they are situated. The United States retail trade generally divides malls into several categories.[6] The small neighborhood malls are usually anchored around a single supermarket, are located on local streets, and serve up to 40 000 people. They are seldom enclosed and often linear in configuration, making them unattractive targets for major terrorist attacks. Community malls add an inexpensive chain store, serve up to 150 000 people from adjacent neighborhoods, and are situated on highway arteries. Regional malls generally have two department stores, a number of specialty shops, and are located at major highway intersections. City center malls are often underground and frequently form part of downtown redevelopment programs. Finally, megamalls combine various combinations of shops, cinemas, restaurants, bars, offices, sports arenas and sometimes amusements parks (as in Mall of America in Minnesota) within one massive structure. In some cases they can form the core of an 'edge city', as with Tyson's Corner in Virginia (Garreau, 1991). These, because of the scale of their activities and their design features, are often seen as the most attractive potential targets for attack.

7.3 MALL SECURITY CONCERNS

While it is impossible to identify and value many of the costs and benefits of securing shopping malls, there are important questions about who should pay the costs if the terrorist threat is to be handled efficiently (Button, 2008).

Shopping malls are generally owned by the private sector and traditionally operators have provided significant amounts of security within their facilities. Indeed, the majority of protection measures at malls is provided by private security companies (Davis et al., 2006). Mall owners and operators have had a vested interest in doing this, and in cooperating with police forces and other private parties (for example, the security personnel employed by individual retailers within a mall and the transportation companies involved in deliveries).

Public confidence in the security of people and property is an important marketing tool for a mall operator. Given the nature of traditional crime, mall operators have the option of passing on some of the risk of any breakdown in this type of security – for example compensation claims – through insurance markets. They can also, as most have done, internalize some of the risk by enhancing their private policing. Indeed, there has been a general increase in private policing in most countries (De Waard, 1999). This is often in part a measure to enhance the secure image of the facility being protected, and in part due to rising external insurance costs.

Both the actions of self-insurance and self-protection, however, throw up the challenges of moral hazard and negative externalities we highlighted earlier in the context of Issac Ehrlich and Gary Becker's work (1972). Self-insurance by a mall, or any retail outlet in it, could mean that the mall or retail outlet may not itself take what may be deemed a reasonable level of precaution against attack.[7] Self-protection, and in particular when it is manifestly clear through signs or other visual indicators that this is in place, has the external impact of making less-protected malls or units more vulnerable. While there are few direct studies of malls in this regard, there is related evidence in support of this diversion effect in the context of surveillance cameras at subway stations where reductions of crime within a station are often significantly offset, by up to 60 percent, by higher rates in the vicinity (Priks, 2015).

But there is also another aspect to this in the case of individual retail units, in that a bombing, or similar attack, on one shop can lead to adjacent ones being physically damaged, and many more suffer economic damage if the overall business of the mall is, due to potential customers' fears, adversely affected for any length of time.

On the premise that they act rationally, shoppers in a mall also have a personal interest in protecting themselves (after all, compensation for being killed by a mugger or shooter is hardly ideal!) and their property, and also often have the option of taking out insurance. Individual shops within malls have differing levels of attraction to criminals and those more susceptible to damage or theft may add additional security.

The threat posed by terrorists is, as we have emphasized, different in that it largely involves uncertainty, with little knowledge about any underlying probability functions, if indeed any exist, rather than risk. The actuarial approach to the challenge is thus far from perfect, and certainly incomplete. The potential costs of a major terrorist incident are also extremely high. Indeed, even Adam Smith, albeit of course not in the context of shopping malls, acknowledged the need for public sector involvement when the financial costs involved in providing an essential economic service exceed the ability of private sector institutions to coordinate funding. These factors make it virtually impossible for a mall operator to either completely insure internally, or through the financial market, against terrorist attacks. This is one reason why Figure 7.2 is very general in its nature. The precise size or shape of any of the facilities shown is virtually impossible to generalize about; the overall layouts vary across malls, entry and exit points, while often needing to meet local safety requirements, are not in any particular pattern, and the location and amount of car parking is site specific.

There is the added problem that a major attack on a mall could have serious and much wider economic and geographical repercussions than those simply relating to the shopping facility. This can be seen and treated as a standard externality problem if these effects have relatively small impacts on overall price levels and incomes in the larger economy, but

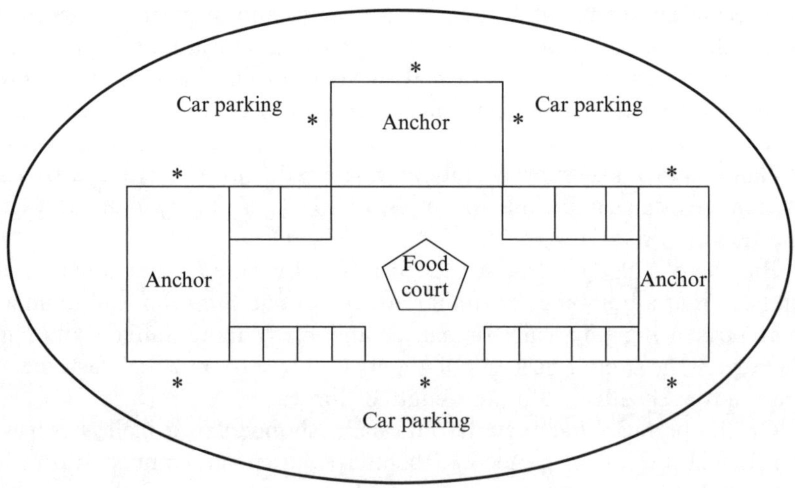

Figure 7.2 Stereotypical United States shopping mall

– and this may well not be the case – if this is not so, the conventional tools of microeconomics break down. The standard *ceteris paribus* assumptions of neoclassical analysis do not hold. The issue becomes one of political risk, although strictly, given the subjective nature of the issue, it is more about political uncertainty.

The extent of these external effects is unclear. In their more general assessment of security threats on urban facilities, that in modern times would include any attacks on shopping malls, Edward Glaeser and Jesse Shapiro (2002) find that from historical experiences of wars and large-scale attacks, essentially the most extreme events, have little impact on the economics of urban form.

The underlying market failures leading to suboptimal security necessitate a degree of public involvement in terms of specifying and, possibly, providing security and, if this fails, resources to cope with many of the effects in the aftermath of an attack. These are obviously not problems unique to mall security but they certainly do exist when it comes to looking at appropriate economic strategies concerning shopping center security.[8] Where the line is drawn between the private sector's responsibilities and those of the public sector is partly a technical one, involving matters of efficiency and effectiveness. In this sense it largely depends on where uncertainty, which is less well handled by the private sector, becomes the dominant concern, but following our earlier discussions in Chapter 4, it often also embodies wider normative judgments involving public perceptions of what the exact role of government should be.

While normally the actual implementation of policies is seen in terms of narrower economic efficiency considerations – essentially the undertaking of a cost–benefit calculation of the effectiveness of public and private actors – when security arises there is often a high degree of subjectivity involving public perceptions.[9] Indicative of this is that, while there is evidence that private security does not reduce security in malls (Gang et al., 1999), many shopping mall operators actively seek a local police presence in their facilities, often a police station, to give added public confidence.

Traditional concerns with security involving theft and attacks on individuals have focused on the location of malls. Older malls located in middle-income groups and accessible only by automobiles were previously considered relatively safe but with increasing suburbanization and changing demographics this is now less the case – 65 percent of United States and Canadian malls of over 400 000 square feet are located in areas with above average crime risk, with 25 percent being in areas having three times or more the national crime risk.[10] Mall design and that of its surrounding area also plays a role in crime rates. Crime tends to be higher in malls with spots that are attractive to juveniles and non-shoppers, and where there are crowded stores offering easy access.

Much of the discussion of mall security and terrorism has relied on anecdotal evidence, perhaps not unexpectedly given the nature of the games that are played with potential terrorists. Their features would seem to make them vulnerable to terrorist attacks of various kinds – they have multiple entrances and exits, are open to the public, have numerous potential places for concealment, often have adjacent car parking, have frequent deliveries, attract numerous shoppers, and employ large numbers of workers. Additionally, since their initial introduction in 1956, many of the larger malls in the US (some 1200 or so) and elsewhere are enclosed with extensive air conditioning and ventilation systems, making them potential targets for toxic chemical or biological attacks. Other developments in the supply chain have seen the greater containerization of consignments reducing considerably the transparency of what is being delivered

A study for the Police Foundation (Davis et al., 2006), funded by the US Justice Department, involving the surveying of 33 state homeland security advisers and 120 security directors of some of the nation's largest indoor shopping centers, as well as visiting eight US malls and two shopping centers in Israel, where security precautions are among the most rigid in the world, sought to assess changes in security since 2001. The survey found that state governments had done little to enhance safety precautions, with only five of the state homeland security officials saying they had provided additional funding to major shopping centers. In addition, only 16 percent of those responsible for the malls examined said that they had increased security-related, self-protection spending beyond the rate of inflation after the terrorist attacks of 11 September 2001.

More than half of the security directors said their officers had received some terrorism-related training, but it was found that the instruction varied in quality and content and 62 percent of the security managers said the anti-terrorism training was inadequate. Additionally, it was found that some shopping centers had 100 percent turnover in security officers each year. High turnover rates of security officers were seen as often undermining the effectiveness of training programs and limiting the institutional reservoir of knowledge, 'At any given time, the security staff includes a good number of new recruits who . . . have not received anything beyond basic company training.'

The most significant gap in emergency preparedness that emerged in the Police Foundation study was a continuing lack of coordination between mall security and separate security in the anchor stores.[11] Only a third of the mall security directors said they rehearsed emergency plans with local law enforcement. None of the malls visited conducted joint exercises with police officers or other first-responders. Such exercises are normally considered important elements for defining clear standards for evaluation of effectiveness. Without them it is impossible to say how well staff would respond in the event of a major incident. The report concluded, 'The private sector generally has not invested in improving security to cope with emergency situations such as a terrorist attack or to protect against petty crimes' (Davis et al., 2006).

7.4 SECURITY MEASURES

Although the US Police Foundation study hardly enthused about the security it found, changes nevertheless have occurred. The problem is that it is very difficult to measure the effectiveness of mall security; referring back to Figure 3.3 in Chapter 3, the benefit curves can only be taken as indicative of form. If there is no attack, this may or may not be due to security measures. Further, if there is a successful attack it is difficult to assess the extent to which security minimized the impacts or thwarted other attacks. Indeed, the fact that there has been no attack but mall security has diverted resources from other, more productive uses may be considered a major victory by terrorists; after all terrorism is not fundamentally about causing material damage, but rather it is intended to demoralize the general population and force it to take actions that it would otherwise have not. There is thus an almost inevitable focus on the nature, scale and cost-effectiveness (the 'C' curve in the figure) when trying to quantify the costs of mall security.

While there are concerns about its scale and detail, as expressed in the Police Foundation report and elsewhere,[12] there have been changes in the ways in which mall security is approached. We focus on the US situation. While initially there was some disjointedness between the public and private sector response to potential attacks on malls, this has gradually been eroded. The US Department of Homeland Security is, for example, now providing shopping center security professionals with information about threats. This was prompted in part by the attacks on London's public transportation system in 2005. David Levenberg of General Growth Properties, which owns or operates more than 200 malls in the US, is cited as saying that the reason for the increased communication is twofold: first, trust levels between private business owners and the DHS have risen in the past year, and second, the agency does not want to be held liable for withholding important information (Smith, 2005).

The major developers of malls have also implemented a variety of new security measures following the September 2001 attacks in the US. For example, the ventilation and heating systems, corridors and parking lots of malls are now more carefully guarded; parking lots are often designed with choke points that funnel cars through areas that cause them to slow down, with some having automatic license plate readers. Bollards and other forms of barrier are now commonplace in front of mall entrances to protect them from being rammed by car or truck bombers. Background checks on security guards are routine, and surveillance cameras are ubiquitous in many countries, both outside and inside malls. Bomb-sniffing dogs are regularly used to sweep malls for explosives akin to the practices at mass transit hubs.

Security staffing, too, has changed in important ways. Previously, security was the job solely of civilian guards but now many malls are patrolled both by police officers and civilian guards. At a more macro level, Westfield America, which owned the leasehold on the mall at New York City's World Trade Center, has created an electronic database containing the blueprints of its 70-plus malls so that if attacked, this information is available to first-responders. As in the UK, where the use of cameras is widespread, many more malls are being equipped with electronic surveillance, often with the aid of federal or state finance.

While there have been considerable advances in the technology surrounding security – developments in surveillance technology, detection equipment and information coordination being perhaps the most germane in the context of shopping malls – the nature of large malls means that there is an inevitable continuing reliance on security personnel. The security labor market has a number of tiers and involves a diversity of skills. Although there have been problems with its quality and with subsequent worker retention,[13] security guard training is still seen as one of the most important elements in attack prevention, and some companies are drawing on the experiences of Israel, a country known for stringent mall security, for guidance. It essentially has a three-cordon approach to security of shopping centers, each involving a different expertise. Briefly, there is a thin outer ring of patrols intended to prevent the more obvious terrorist acts; then there is a check on mall entry akin to, but more rigorous than that normally found at airports, and then there are internal patrols trained to look for suspicious behavior inside the mall.

Mall design and refurbishments are also being modified to take account of potential terrorist attacks. While more modern shopping centers were already technically quite well designed to prevent crime with good lighting, wide corridors, few public places that could allow concealment, the ability to isolate areas, and so on, these features, and additional ones, such as the location of parking places and the design of parking decks, are being emphasized in designing the next generation of malls.

All these actions by the private sector are obviously not costless and those supported by state funding, such as additional policing and improved communications systems, must be added to the costs borne by taxpayers in providing public security. The amount developers are spending on mall security varies, but it is generally about $1.30 per square foot, although it can be far more, depending on the size, design and location of the mall. Westfield America, for example, spends $40 million a year – amounting to about 20 percent of operating costs – on security (Smith, 2005). Such costs also do not take into account any adverse affects on business that may result if they impinge on the 'shopping experience' of customers for example in terms of searches and surveillance.

7.5 CONCLUDING THOUGHTS

In an age of widespread automobile ownership, shopping malls in their various guises are important elements in the transportation value chain that links movements of goods to retailers and then from retailers to final consumption, the ultimate last mile in the jargon of supply management. They are also influential in forming the local human geography, often being at the center of interactions that extend well beyond shopping.

It is not easy to protect shopping malls from terrorist attack; by their nature they have generally been constructed to facilitate easy access for the various groups that use them; they are often viewed as de facto public spaces. They are a classic case of a soft target in TSA terms, especially as security in many other parts of the transportation supply chain has been enhanced, making them more difficult to attack successfully.

While there has been a certain amount of managerial and accounting analysis of the problems of mall security, and discussion of the role of the public sector, as with many other security topics the economics dimension has been largely neglected. In particular, the potential implications of self-protection and self-insurance by various stakeholders, and government's role in overseeing this, have been given only a small amount of attention, but this essentially institutional question seems important.

NOTES

1. For an account of the growth of wider academic interest in supply chain security and a review of some of the recent work in the area, see Gould et al. (2010). The security of shopping malls has many similarities to the issues involved in similar physical entities such as sports arenas. The analysis of the latter has some relevance here, although much of the analysis relates more to conventional crime rather than terrorist activities; see for example, Baker et al. (2007) and Campaniello (2012).

2. While mall-based crimes are not discussed in detail, the focus being on terrorism, there is inevitably some degree of overlap in the types of strategies that may be adopted.
3. There is also increased concern about other forms of major assault at malls. For example, a bombing took place in October 2002 in Vantaa, Finland in a local Myyrmanni shopping mall, killing seven people and injuring 166. The possibility of the bomber having links to any radical groups or terrorist organizations was ruled out.
4. In some cases the costs of protecting malls have, however, been high. Pressed for additional troops to police the Iraqi 2005 general elections, the US Pentagon dispatched 30 000 shopping mall security guards to the troubled Sunni Triangle region.
5. In this sense, and referring back to Figure 3.3, the various related cost and benefit functions may not be smooth but have kinks in them, producing various thresholds where shoppers are particularly sensitive; see Hardy (2007).
6. For an alternative set of definitions see Australian Government Attorney-General's Department (2006).
7. There is a difference here between the mall owner and the shop owner. The act of self-insurance by the mall owner endogenizes the costs of a potential attack on the mall, and with it confers an external benefit on retailers within the mall. Self-protection by a retailer means that the overall likelihood of attack on the mall is treated by the retailer as exogenous, with that on the individual business as endogenous.
8. For a general discussion of the issues that emerge in government becoming involved in the protection of private property, see Litan and Orszag (2002).
9. This was seen in the debates in the US over whether private operators should implement new airport security measures after the 2001 terrorist attacks or whether they should be carried out by a federal agency. More generally, after the events of 11 September a number of states, including California, Illinois and Michigan, initiated a more stringent regulation of private security.
10. Crime risk here is defined in terms of the CAP Index – see www.capindex.com.
11. In the sense that overall mall security may be seen as a public good, the lack of involvement and of self-protection by the individual retailers and offices may be taken as a free-rider problem. What is often absent from the information we have on insurance is that regarding the policies that individual stores and offices may have. Lohse et al.'s (2012) theoretical analysis suggests that: 'the presence of market insurance decreases the efficient provision level of the public good, since fully insured individuals behave as if they were risk neutral'.
12. The media also periodically make assessments of various aspects of mall security, and these have often also been unfavorable; for example, see Hall (2003) and Erman (2002).
13. Robert Davis et al. (2006) point to the low wages in the private security sector coupled with poor career prospects as the major factors causing this.

8. Maritime security

The existence of the sea means the existence of pirates
Malayan Proverb

8.1 INTRODUCTION

Maritime transportation, defined as ports, waterways and their intermodal connectors, carries about 80 percent of international trade by volume according to the United Nations. It has also, as far as historic records go, always been a target for attack. Although this has in the past largely been for commercial gain, basically piracy, rather than to terrorize larger populations, the listing of some acts of piracy seen in Box 2.1 highlights diversity in the motivations of pirates and the changing motivations for attacks.

As we see, while much of this activity has been for the personal financial benefits of the individual perpetrators, there has also been a tradition of institutional piracy that has enjoyed some forms of state support.[1] More recently these acts of piracy have been supplemented by concerns that ships may be used to deliver various weapons of mass destruction, carry hostile operatives ('Trojan Horses') or, contraband, or be destroyed as a terror threat to populations. In terms of the potential for carrying hostile operatives, for example, ten people were killed and 16 wounded on 14 March 2004 in a double suicide bombing at Israel's Ashdod Port when two Palestinian suicide bombers hid behind a false wall in a 50-foot container and succeeded in infiltrating the port. The first suicide bomber blew himself up close to a group of workers standing next to a machine repair workshop, killing five people. The second detonated his bomb near the outer fence on the sidewalk in a storage and refrigeration area.

Additionally, given the increase in global specialization and the emergence of extended global supply chains, disruption to maritime trade can potentially have serious economic implications.[2] Estimates of these costs are inevitably contextual but Gordon et al. (2006) put a figure of about $45 billion for a dirty bomb attack on a major US port. The calculations relating to a full nuclear attack on a port, partially due to higher levels of uncertainty, vary considerably but ABT Associates (2003) suggest direct trade losses to the United States would be around \$100 to \$200 billion, with additional property damage of between \$50 and \$500 billion. Overall, the study estimates indirect costs to the economy ranging from \$300 billion to \$1.4 trillion, with casualties of between 50 000 and 1 000 000.

Table 8.1 provides a listing of some key incidents that highlight the diverse nature of more recent maritime attacks, and Table 8.2 details the temporal pattern of attacks on ports between 1968 and 2007.[3]

The 11 September 2001 attacks in the US brought to the forefront longer-standing concerns about the vulnerability of transportation to terrorist attack. It also, although less overtly, suggested to the authorities the possibility that terrorists could severely disrupt the global supply chain by using shipping containers or vessels to attack population centers or critical infrastructure. Much of the security debate and many of the counter-terrorism initiatives have to date focused on aviation and surface passenger modes, primarily because these have been used in most of the actual attacks – for example, bombs on buses in the UK and Israel and on trains in Spain as well as aircraft in the US. Passenger modes have the potential for inflicting casualties both on those using them as well as third parties, and this is highly visible. This does not mean that freight transportation has escaped attack – the introduction of anthrax into the US mail system being an example – but events have been less numerous. The potential for concealing a large weapon of mass destruction, either a platform for its direct use or as a means of movement to a specific location, in a container is, however, viewed as a major threat.

Achieving a secure container supply chain, as we saw in Chapter 2, poses significant policy challenges, given the complexity and international nature of much of the business. The maritime transportation of containers, whether domestic or international, is part of a larger complex global supply structure that involves numerous actors located on different continents. A typical voyage of a maritime shipping container can involve up to 25 actors, generate 30 to 40 documents, use two or three modes of transportation, and physically is handled at up to 15 locations. To give some idea of the scale of the system, there are over 4000 ports in the world, although 20 account for about 45 percent of the world's throughput of containers. This geographic concentration on a small number of large ports has significant policy implications. Putting any one port out of action could have severe consequences for global trade.

In terms of actors, non-bulk cargo enters the container supply chain by being palletized and placed in shipping containers by its manufacturers or an intermediary forwarder. Transportation firms convey the loaded containers to ports where they are cleared by customs and

Table 8.1 Some acts of maritime terrorism

Date	Location	Event
June 1968	Galveston, US	Japanese vessel *Mikagasan Maru* damaged by a bomb allegedly placed by Cuban exiles.
March 1973	Lebanon	Greek charter *Sanya* sank in Beirut by explosion by Black September Organization.
December 1973	Miami, US	Two bombs damaged the cargo ship *Mereghan II* while waiting to lift cargo in Miami River docks.
March 1974	France	Pierre Overnay brigade attacked the barge *Ouest France* while moored alongside a quay and firebombed 180 cars.
July 1974	Belfast, UK	Bomb planted by Provisional IRA exploded on the ferry *Ulster Queen*.
November 1975	San Juan, Puerto Rico	Russian vessel privateers damaged by bomb blasts while at anchor in the port.
August 1976	Lebanon	Greek vessel *Tina* sunk by limpet mines planted by right-wing Lebanese Christians.
September 1976	Port Elizabeth, US	Soviet cargo vessel damaged by a limpet mine planted by an anti-Castro refugee.
October 1976	Lebanon	Greek vessels *Eko*, *Riri* and *Spiro* sunk in port by limpet mines.
October 1978	Israel	Israeli Navy sank a bomb-laden Fatah vessel heading for Eilat with intent on destroying the Eilat–Ashkelon pipeline and oil tank farms in the port.
October 1980	Genoa, Italy	Libyan vessel almost sank after a limpet mine explosion; Maltese National Front suspected.
February 1983	Lough Foyle, UK	British cargo vessel seized in an inlet by IRA and the ship blown up.
June 1984	Buenos Aires, Argentina	Tankers *Perito Morena* and *Belgrano* set ablaze by the Sargento Cisneros Commandos.
September 1985	Cyprus	PLO's Force-17 seized an Israeli yacht on Yom Kippur and killed three on board.
October 1985	Egypt	Italian cruise vessel *Achille Lauro* seized with 511 passengers on board by 4 members of the Popular Front for the Liberation of Palestine; a US passenger killed.
January 1986	Messina, Italy	Two 135-tonne Cypriot-flagged hydrofoils were bombed and sunk while docked for repairs.
January 1987	Mauritania	Panamanian bulker *Maritime King* attacked with rocket fire by Polisario guerrillas.
July 1994	Jijel, Algeria	GIA attackers boarded a cargo vessel moored in the port; seven Italian sailors killed.

Table 8.1 (continued)

Date	Location	Event
April 1996	Colombo, Sri Lanka	Van Ommeren docked vessel came under mortar attack by 2 LTTE gunboats.
September 1997	Trincomalee, Sri Lanka	LTTE attack vessel *Athena* with a limpet mine while at anchor.
October 2002	Aden, Yemen	French tanker *Limburg* attacked by a suicide boat; one sailor drowned.
June 2004	Gwadar, Pakistan	Chinese engineers developing deep-sea port came under rocket attack.
August 2005	Lamitan, Philippines	Bomb exploded among the LPG tanks on the ferry *Dona Ramona* injuring at least 30.
March 2007	Ambon, Indonesia	Bomb exploded at the port gates in the Yos Sudarso port in Ambon.
September 2007	Dellys, Algeria	Coast Guard troops targeted by suicide truck bomber during a flag-raising ceremony.

Table 8.2 Global maritime terrorist attacks in ports (1968–2007)

Year	Attacks	Year	Attacks	Year	Attacks	Year	Attacks	Year	Attacks
1968	2	1970	1	1980	3	1990	0	2000	1
1969	0	1971	1	1981	2	1991	0	2001	1
		1972	2	1982	4	1992	0	2002	1
		1973	2	1983	2	1993	1	2003	2
		1974	6	1984	5	1994	1	2004	3
		1975	5	1985	2	1995	1	2005	1
		1976	3	1986	2	1996	2	2006	1
		1977	1	1987	3	1997	4	2007	2
		1978	2	1988	3	1998	0		
		1979	2	1989	0	1999	0		

Source: Talas and Menachof (2014).

loaded onto a ship. The containers then are transported to a final destination port where they are cleared by customs and transported to their final purchasers or distributors. A container, during its voyage through the global supply chain, may also be placed in temporary storage for extended periods of time as it waits for the availability of further transport.

The maritime segment of the global container supply chain involves a hub-and-spoke system of ports and shipping services. Such systems offer major commercial benefits in the form of economies of scale, scope and density. To benefit from scale benefits ports and maritime operators maintain capital-intensive operations and place a heavy emphasis on increasing the amount of containers they handle. Economics of scope occur when firms can spread their costs by offering a range of services. Economies of density occur when the presence of a network hub results in average revenue increases that are greater than the number of services provided. Countering this, there are some, such as Hendricks and Singhal (2005), who argue that this approach, which leads to single sourcing, low inventories and buffer stocks, and limited flexibility, increases the vulnerability of the supply chain to attack, and intensifies the potential effects of any such attacks.

The operations of the world's ports and maritime operators are interdependent and interact with the rest of the container supply chain. A lack of security at one port, at the maritime operator's facilities or on ships may expose other ports and maritime operators and other firms in the supply chain to security risks. A terrorist attack on a container port or on the facilities of a maritime operator may damage critical infrastructure and result in a costly disruption of the container supply chain. A container-based terrorist attack could have the effect of shutting down, or dramatically slowing down, the supply chain. This could occur when government officials and private firms face uncertainty in not knowing how many container-based attacks are being considered (Flynn, 2004). Therefore, they would be likely to take preemptive and precautionary actions to ensure the security of the entire container supply chain.

Institutional problems pose particular challenges at the international level. For example, the US does not have jurisdiction over foreign firms, containers or vessels until they reach American waters. It also does not have the resources to guarantee the security of every container arriving at a US port. The response of the US government, like all others, to global terrorism is seen, therefore, as needing to be measured and coordinated. There are potentially large opportunity costs in not doing so.

There are, however, trade-offs between security and efficiency, as Kevin Hendricks and Vinod Singhal (2005) highlight. Programs involving full inspection of containers are, given current technology, highly resource-intensive. As argued in Chapter 3, while inadequate security is costly, so is an excessive emphasis on security that offsets the economic benefits gained from trade liberalization, containerization, container tracking technology and management information systems. It is a standard economic issue of opportunity costs.

8.2 THE ISSUES AND INTERNATIONAL REACTIONS

Maritime containers are the primary mode of transport for international trade in manufactured products and parts. There are some 34 million containers in the world, with ports such as Shanghai, Singapore, Shenzhen and Hong Kong each handling over 25 million TEUs (twenty-foot equivalent units) in 2013. Of the US ports, only Los Angeles (18th), Long Beach (20th) and New York/New Jersey (26th) are within the top 30 in the world. Port congestion has, however, become an issue, with delays on the US West Coast creating problems for US cargo interests. As rigorous security programs suggest that even more delay will accrue as port congestion grows in the coming years, the views of cargo owners with respect to security programs and security costs become relevant in any risk management program planning.

Not only is global trade involving containers focusing on specific routings, the business is continuing to consolidate in the hands of a few lines. The top ten container carriers offered 45 percent of the slots available in 2003 (the top 20 offered 64.4 percent), and concentration of the market has continued with more mergers and acquisitions; in 2004 the top 20 offered 70.5 percent of the slots available (Containerisation International, 2006). Although it looks as though the number of actors is small, this is far from the case. A European study concluded that 21 different actors are involved in a container chain in addition to the buyer and seller (European Conference of Ministers of Transport, 2004).

Container integrity is key to the success of containerization in the post-Second World War era; prior to its advent, theft from ports, terminals and ships was a significant commercial risk, as was damage to cargoes. Today, international shipping lines face the additional uncertainty that terrorists will use the vessel or the container as a weapon of mass destruction, while ports face, at minimum, congestion in anticipation, during or after an incident, and at worst, devastation.

8.3 INTERNATIONAL INITIATIVES

In response to the terrorist acts of September 2001, although the other events outlined earlier also played a role, multilateral regulators and more specific national initiatives led to the implementation of new maritime security requirements. The approach of international agencies such as the International Maritime Organization has largely been to find areas where generic measures may be useful in enhancing security. The role of such agencies is essentially seen as being to retain credibility in the oversight role they perform and to initiate rules that do not impose excessive costs on the overall system. There is a practical need not to overstretch the resources of the poorer members of the maritime community. This by its nature means designing a strategy that meets the needs of the most competitive markets where there are limited resources available. Inevitably, flexibility is deemed important.

The UN's International Maritime Organization (IMO) has thus effectively taken the model used in international aviation security oversight to structure an institutional response to the terrorist threat. The ICAO policy has been to establish oversight guidelines that Member States agree to adopt. Given the diversity of air transportation markets around the world, ranging from totally free markets to institutionalized monopolies, and the resources available in each country, the ICAO has sought to allow local variations in the exact detail of implementation. The IMO's International Ship and Port Facility Security Code (ISPS) essentially replicates the international airline model.

In broad terms, the ISPS Code requires individual governments to assess the risks facing their ports and establishes a three-tiered security system in which Level 1 is associated with normal level of security threats, Level 2 with medium level of security threats, and Level 3 with high level of security threats. The Code requires that, as a minimum, ports, maritime operators and ship owners establish security plans that correspond with the three security levels. These security plans should indicate the operational and physical measures required to comply with the three security levels. They must also designate security officers who are responsible for ensuring that their facility or their organization's facilities comply with the requirements associated with each maritime security level. Finally, they may have to obtain and operate the specific types of equipment needed to meet the security level requirements.[4]

In more detail, in December 2002, the International Maritime Organization (2002b) developed the International Ship and Port Facility Security Code (ISPS Code) and added it as an amendment to the *Safety of Life at Sea, 1974* (a widely-adopted UN Convention) to address concerns about vessel safety. The Code sets forth mandatory security requirements to be met by governments, ports, shipping companies and terminal operators to enhance the security of the world's maritime transportation system. The US implemented the ISPS Code by passing the *Maritime Transportation Security Act of 2002* with effect 1 July 2004. The International Labor Organization passed the *Seafarers' Identity Documents Convention (Revised), 2003 (No. 185)* so that standards are set for a biometric feature – a fingerprint – on this globally recognized document and national security agencies can ensure these mobile workers are who they claim.

Consistency of data is important for security analysis, and on the cargo side, the World Customs Organization (WCO) (2002) has adopted the *Resolution of the Customs Co-operation Council on Security and Facilitation of the International Trade Supply Chain* to facilitate this. Since then, the WCO has developed a package of measures, including: an amended data model and a list of essential data elements for identification of high-risk consignments; customs guidelines for Advance Cargo Information to enable the pre-arrival electronic transmission of customs data; WCO Guidelines for Co-operative Arrangements between Members and Private Industry to Increase Supply Chain Security and Facilitate the Flow of International Trade; and an International Convention on Mutual Administrative Assistance in Customs Matters to assist members in developing a legal basis to support these initiatives. The objective of these measures was to develop a framework of standards that would encourage the facilitation of seamless trade, and which could be applied consistently across customs jurisdictions (World Customs Organization, 2005).

These various measures, and those initiated by individual countries under their own volition, have not been costless. First, there are the direct costs that are passed onto shippers in the form of implicit fees. These vary considerably by country and by facilities within countries, but Table 8.3 provides an indication of the transparent elements of the costs of additional port security across a range of western economies. There are then the less transparent costs that the ports embrace within their normal charges as part of the overhead costs, and that are indirectly passed to port users on these charges. Finally, the security measures, and especially regulations, can impose operational costs on the users of maritime infrastructure that can delay movements and add to the uncertainty of the service that can be provided.

More detailed estimates have been made regarding the costs of dealing with the Somali pirate attacks (Table 8.4). While not allocated explicitly to shipping companies or government, they do highlight the diversity of costs involved in securing the maritime sea-lanes where the pirates have made their attacks. Looked at from another perspective, Alexa Sullivan (2010) produces figures specifically in relation to the Suez Canal, and estimates that piracy in 2009 disrupted about $7.4 billion of goods traded. The reactions of shipping companies incur costs by rerouting to avoid hazardous areas, thereby incurring higher sailing costs, but keeping insurance costs down, adopting non-conventional weapons such as electronic fences, arming vessels with security teams and magnetic acoustic devices, paying higher insurance premiums and thus transferring risk.

Table 8.3 Variations across port container security charges (2012–2014)

Example of average terminal security fees		$/TEU
Australian ports		7.50
Europe	Belgian ports	10.98
	Denmark	15.00
	Dutch ports	10.86
	French ports	12.33
	Italian ports	9.76
	Latvian ports	7.32
	Norwegian ports	2.44
	Spanish ports	6.71
	Irish ports	8.54
	Swedish ports	
	Gothenburg	3.95
	Heisingburg	2.63
	Turkish ports	12.00
	UK ports	
	Felixstowe	19 for import & 10 for export
	Harwich	19 for import & 10 for export
	Thames port	19 for import & 10 for export
	Tilbury	12.70
US	Charleston	7.00
	Houston	8.00
	Miami	7.00
	Long Beach	5.00
Others	Shenzhen	6.25
	Hong Kong	2.58

Sources: Adapted from Bichou (2014) and https://www.hapag-lloyd.com/en/news/surcharges.html.

8.4 US SECURITY POLICY

To supplement these multilateral efforts, and to take account of local priorities and challenges, many national initiatives were put in train. The US, for example, implemented advance notification rules, and launched a series of programs, including Operation Safe Commerce, the Container Security Initiative (CSI), the Customs–Trade Partnership against Terrorism (C-TPAT) and Free and Secure Trade (FAST). These cover various elements of the international maritime supply chain; see Figure 8.1. These should be set within the existing, albeit more limited, Maritime Transportation Security Act (MTSA) of 2002, and the IMO initiated International Port

Table 8.4 Cost components of Somali piracy (2011–2012)

	Cost in 2011	Cost in 2012
Ransoms	\$160 million	\$63.5 million
Military operations	\$1.27 billion	\$1.09 billion
Security equipment and guards	\$1.064 – \$1.16 billion	\$1.65 – \$2.06 billion
Rerouting	\$486 – \$681 million	\$290.5 million
Increased speed	\$2.71 billion	\$1.53 billion
Cost to labor	\$195 million	\$471.6 million
Prosecutions and imprisonments	\$16.4 million	\$14.89 million
Insurance	\$635 million	\$550.7 million
Counter-piracy organizations	\$21.3 million	\$24.08 million
Total cost	\$6.6 – \$6.9 billion	\$5.7 – \$6.1 billion

Source: Bellish (2013); Bowden and Basnet (2012).

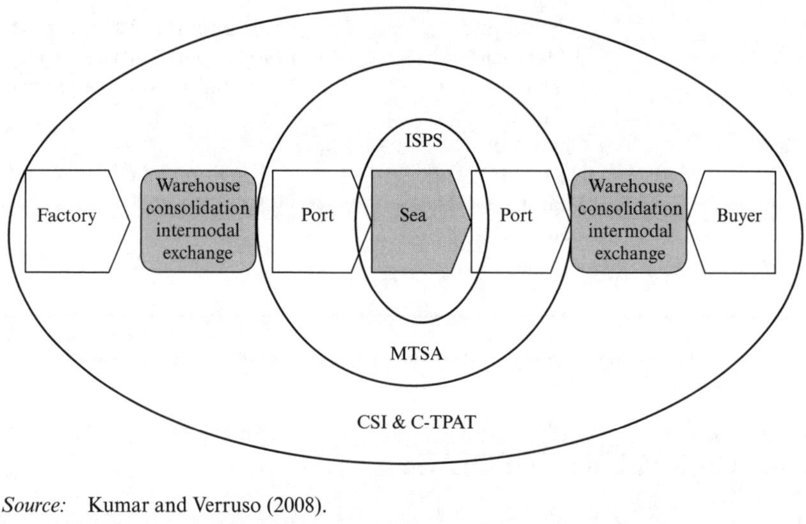

Source: Kumar and Verruso (2008).

Figure 8.1 Maritime transfer points showing domains of ISPS, MTSA, CSI and C-TPAT

and Security Code (ISPS), both of which cover maritime port and vessel procedures, and have security mandates regarding infrastructure, security personnel, emergency contingency plans and training programs.

Operation Safe Commerce acts as a test bed for piloting new procedures and technologies throughout the supply chain. The CSI focuses on the container; through bilateral agreements with other countries, it places US customs officials in foreign ports as part of pre-screening processes, and allows container inspection to US standards to occur in foreign ports. There are 58 ports participating in the CSI and the traffic passing through them constitutes about 80 percent of US maritime cargo trade.

The C-TPAT program aims to make security a cooperative activity throughout the cargo supply chain. Official guidelines are implemented by registered companies and built into their contracts with their trading partners. Initiated in 2001 with seven large firms, by 2014 it had 10 854 members, of which 4315 accounted for 45 percent of imports into the US. Only American companies, however, may belong. The sole exception is Mexican manufacturers in *maquiladoras*; other foreign companies have been admitted by virtue of getting their US operations certified.[5] The economic benefits associated with voluntary participation in C-TPAT include firms enjoying faster and fewer document inspections at ports and significantly fewer examinations of cargo. In the event of a container-based terrorist incident, participants in C-TPAT will also normally be allowed to resume operations faster than non-participants.

Looking at these, and other initiatives, Booz Allen Hamilton (2003) argue that security can seldom be viewed as a point problem, with threats concentrated at one location, but rather one that involves protecting, in this case, the flow of international maritime trade. Links are usually controlled by one corporate entity – ship, rail line, road – and vulnerability is normally greater at nodes because containers are least vulnerable in motion, particularly on the high seas where they may be inaccessible. Land border delays increase vulnerability for trucks that must sit and wait. As a result, ships are generally perceived to be more secure than railways; they, in turn, are seen as generally more secure than trucks. This does raise questions about whether the exact form of devolving security responsibilities applied to US maritime trade can be applied across all modes, especially since to date there has been no major testing of the C-TPAT approach.

8.5 THE PRIVATE SECTOR AND US SECURITY POLICIES

As we have seen regarding other modes, there are often commercial incentives for transportation suppliers to ensure their activities are secure, and this holds for maritime movements. There are also issues of how the private sector reacts to official policies. The private actors in the container-based supply chain differ, not only between the various elements in the chain, but also within each element. The large, multinational enterprises have diverse objectives, resource bases and structures, and their involvements in the chain can vary considerably. In consequence their approaches to security differ (Li et al., 2005). At the other extreme, suppliers of first or last mile links are often small players that enter and leave markets and thus have unknown track records. Finally, if a container is determined to be at risk and it is deep in the hold of a ship, accessing it can put a port at risk. It is against this background that the US sought to move the problem of identifying containers at risk offshore through the CSI and advance notification requirements built into the Maritime Transportation Security Act, 2002.

As explained earlier, terrorism security activities embrace the prevention and deterrence of an incident, the short-term response to it, and the longer-term remediation and recovery from an incident when one does occur. Much of the focus, however, has traditionally been on the first of these; to quote Henry Willis and David Ortiz (2004),

> Both public and private sector initiatives to improve the security of the global supply chain have focused largely on preventing and deterring smuggling and terrorist attacks . . . Few initiatives have focused on improving the fault tolerance or resilience of the system, which could be a fruitful area for new security measures.

The industry response to security is also based on the way safety has been handled. As in other sectors, this has generally involved the development of risk management techniques and processes built on incidents with measurable probability for the private insurance market to assess in setting premiums. The new post-11 September security environment, while it still addresses these, now means that companies must prepare for and remediate terrorism, in a climate of uncertainty, and one with insufficient incidents for measuring probability. A regulatory policy of 'implement and amend', as it currently exists in the US, adds to, rather than reduces, the uncertainty that cargo owners face. Add to this the US policy approach of mandating action without allocated funding, and more uncertainty is created. Additionally, as we have seen, some elements of security are not only private goods, but have public good elements; as Sean Gorman (2005) notes: private markets lead to public vulnerabilities.

The attitudes and the approaches of the private sector are, therefore, important in influencing how official policies are formulated, affecting the *de jure* element, and in the ways they will work in practice, affecting the de facto element. The cargo industry, weighing up the costs and benefits of the situation, has largely been supportive of US security initiatives, both within the US and in international forums like the WCO. The World Shipping Council (WSC), the International Mass Retail Association (IMRA) and the National Industrial Transportation League (NITL), and their member companies, have supported the *Maritime Transportation Security Act of 2002* and its 24-hour rule, the Container Security Initiative, and the C-TPAT program as well as the 'development and implementation of analogous efforts at the international level through the World Customs Organization . . . The industry strongly supports the governments of trading nations establishing predictable and transparent, and mutually consistent, security rules governing these issues' (World Shipping Council et al., 2003).

There are, however, few studies looking at how the maritime supplying firms have responded to these factors, and what differs somewhat in their findings, in part because of the size of the undertakings examined.

Brooks and Button (2007), look at a sample of ten companies in the top 100 that imported goods to the US, or exported goods from it, and three cargo industry associations and found evidence of pre-emptive action in the sector before government measures were introduced. Many of the companies, for example, had already reduced the number of transportation suppliers or contracted with carriers offering larger geographic scope in the 1990s to gain greater control or minimize supply chain costs, and after September 2001 reduction programs continued. For manufacturers and retailers, the key focus before 2001 was the integrity of their supply chain to deal with issues of intrusive theft and theft of whole containers and the period after 2001 was to a large extent an extension of this. The vast majority said they were not switching to outsourcing distribution/ logistics (Table 8.5). The majority also indicated that they required their transport companies to be C-TPAT participants.

The authors found it difficult to quantify the economic impacts of regulations within global supply chains as companies had been either reluctant to share their data for proprietary and security reasons or had not been able to quantify costs. Only five companies were willing to discuss the costs of enhanced security, four claiming it to be less than 1 percent and one that it was 1 percent The others argued that it was hard to quantify but as

Table 8.5 Strategic responses to changed security environment

Strategic Response	Number	Frequency
Require C-TPAT of transport suppliers	10	7
Added requirements to transport contracts	10	6
Outsourced transportation and distribution	10	0
New terms of trade	10	1
Neither outsourced nor new terms of sale	10	9
Dropped markets	9	1

requirements become standardized and a uniform cost for all companies it would produce a level competitive playing field. The cost of security, however, was not a key pressure point for many of the companies.

A somewhat different result emerges in a study of 16 US port authorities and terminal operators, 15 container lines, and three security consultants by Mark Thibault et al. (2006), which found the scale of operations generally made it easier for small operators to make investments needed to comply with the new requirements, but they did question why they need to conform to the same physical security standards as much larger ports when their operations tend to be much more limited and often more specific. From a business perspective, they found it harder to spread fixed costs of standard requirements across a smaller base.

Moving outside of the US, SITPRO (2005) has concluded that, overall, the cost of implementing compliance with the ever-increasing volume of regulations is escalating. While developed countries have the ability to provide companies with some financial assistance – for example Export Development Canada's Security Compliance Loan program (Brown, 2006) – the cost of implementing security programs and maintaining their validity may simply be impossible to achieve in poorer countries. This raises the question about whether support should be expanded under the umbrella of World Bank and other multilateral agency funding. The Bank already gives limited funding to help some countries meet international security commitments – for example, in 2006 two International Development Association credits and two grants for a combined total of $33.57 million for Burkina Faso, Cameroon, Guinea and Mali.

8.6 TO BUNDLE OR UNBUNDLE? US CARGO PREFERENCE

We now turn to consider the implications of linking security policy with other policy objectives, basically creating a joint product that bundles services (Chen and Chiu, 2010). In the case of aviation, the US Civilian Reserve Air Force (CRAF), whereby US airlines have a monopoly of government travel to ensure that airlift is available at times of national need, is one example. Here we look at the US cargo preference policy that stipulates that part of food aid has to be shipped in US vessels to ensure maritime capacity when needed. The commercial fleet is being treated, at least in part, as a reserve of security capacity, and this, like the CRAF program, has economic implications (Lewis, 1998).

The cargo preference regime is designed to favor the use of the nation's merchant fleet. It dates back to the Cargo Preference Act of 1954, and in 2015 required at least 50 percent of the gross tonnage of cargoes procured, furnished or financed by the US government to be transported on privately owned, US-flag commercial vessels to the extent such vessels are available at fair and reasonable rates. International food assistance provided by the US Agency for International Development (USAID) and the US Department of Agriculture (USDA) is included in the definition of government-generated cargo.

Between 1954 and 1985, 50 percent of US food aid had to be shipped using US-flag vessels. This rose to 75 percent between 1985 and 2012, before reverting back to 50 percent. US registered ships do not have to be US built but the officers and pilots must be US citizens or permanent residents, as must 75 percent of the rest of the crew. Given the high pay scale of US maritime workers, this policy has led to a significant decline in the US-flagged fleet. According to the US Maritime Administration, in 1955 there were 1072 vessels sailing internationally under the US flag, but this has declined to about 80 vessels, 2 percent of the world's tonnage. In contrast there were 794 US-owned vessels registered, often under a flag of convenience, in other countries in 2010. The US-flag fleet is heavily dependent on cargo preference traffic; for example in 2008 preference cargoes accounted for 49.6 percent of that carried (Subcommittee On Coast Guard and Maritime Transportation, US House of Representatives, 2010).

In terms of immediate security needs, the Maritime Security Program provides annual funding of $186 million to support a fleet of 60 commercial vessels that are available to the US government in times of war or national emergency, with the 1920 Jones Act giving US-flag ships that are US-owned and built, a monopoly of domestic shipping trade. US registered ships carry 100 percent of military cargo, in addition to that moved as part of food aid programs.[6]

Because of the high costs of US-flag vessels, the Food Security Act of 1985 required the US Maritime Administration (MARAD) to reimburse USAID and USDA for any extra expense in using them, and for any amount by which the cost of ocean transportation exceeded 20 percent of the cost of food purchases and ocean transportation costs. The 2013 Budget eliminated the requirement that MARAD reimburse USAID and USDA for 'excess freight' costs.

We are concerned with the effect this direction of food aid to the US flag fleet, essentially for security reasons, may have on US aid policy, focusing on the economic implications, broadly defined, of moving back to a 75 percent minimum use of this fleet for carriage of USAID and USDA food aid. The US House of Representatives passed the Coast Guard and

Table 8.6 Cargo preference carriage (1 October 2013 to 30 September 2014 in current $)

	US Flag	Foreign Flag	Total	Percentage US
Bulker	260 810	144 110	404 920	64.4%
Liner	164 468	121 549	286 017	57.5%
Tanker	0	0	0	0
Total	425 278	265 659	690 937	61.6% (weighted average)

Source: https://forums.info.usaid.gov/index.php?q=topic/cargo-preference-statistics-dated-june-09-2014.

Maritime Transportation Act of 2014, which included a provision to increase cargo preference for food aid programs to 75 percent, although this was subsequently removed from the final Act.

Food aid is a small part of the maritime trade of the US. In 2013 it amounted to 510 shipments, totaling 1.3 million tonnes, at an ocean carriage cost of $212.2 million, and involved 41 ships. Nine ships handled 81 percent of the aid moved, with six of the dry bulk carriers accounting for 52 percent.[7] Liberty Maritime Corporation (49 percent), Sealift of Delaware (20 percent) and Maersk Inc. (18 percent) dominated the tonnage moved, with Liberty and Sealift each using four ships while Maersk employed 14, with four of these accounting for more than 90 percent of the food aid it carried. Overall, despite the limits drawn up by the legislated minimum of 50 percent carriage by US registered vessels, the fleet carries more than this (Table 8.6).[8]

The conditions for US registry push up the costs of such vessels. The US Maritime Administration (2011) finds that the average cost of operating a US registered ship is 2.7 times that of a foreign flag equivalent vessel, a difference largely accounted for by the much higher proportion of labor costs associated with US registry (Figure 8.2) linked with the union-based wage rates paid to US mariners.

The debates surrounding cargo preference largely revolve around the conflicting needs of retaining maritime capacity for security reasons and for supporting the US's food aid program. A few stylized facts highlight the trade-off issues. In Figure 8.3 there are two outcomes of expenditure – explicitly security and aid – and a fixed public budget. There are externalities involved in the sense that providing shipping explicitly for security will also make some amount of capacity available for aid transportation and vice versa. Assuming there are no scale effects, and the positive

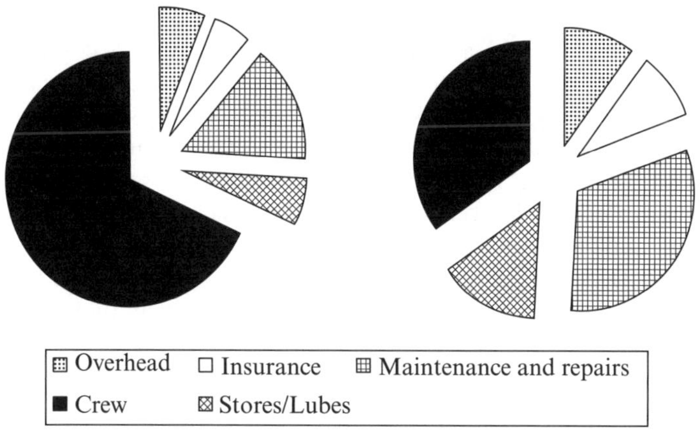

Source: US Maritime Administration (2011).

Figure 8.2 Breakdown of US (left) and foreign-flagged (right) shipping costs

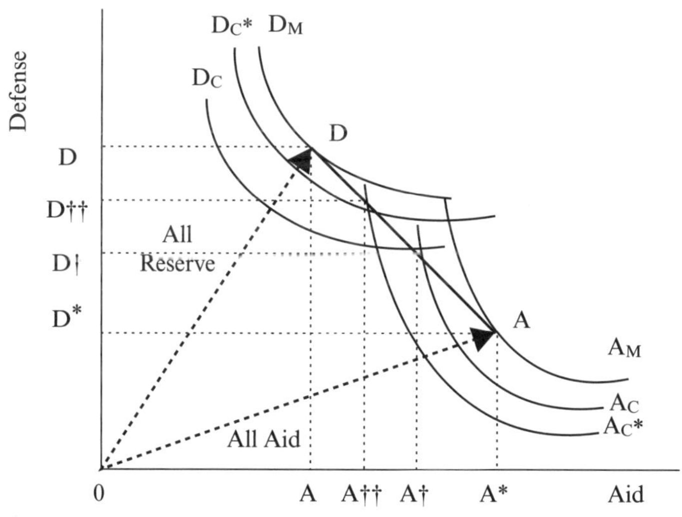

Figure 8.3 The aid/ security trade-off

externalities between the two policies are constant ratios, then if the public funds go to maintaining a military reserve fleet, given its costs, this will lead to point **D** being realized on the highest obtainable preference curve D_M, with D security and A aid being provided. If all is spent on food aid, then the outcome will be at point **A**, proving A* of aid and D* of security.

The problem starts when there are two groups in society, one having a strong preference for security (as represented by the D indifference mapping) and the other with a strong food aid preference (the A mapping). Since both **D** and **A** are unobtainable concurrently, a judgment must be made either favoring those with a strong defense bias or those with a strong food aid bias.

There are of course intermediate possibilities, as under the existing situation in the US, at points on the line between **D** and **A** with public expenditure shared between explicit defense and food aid programs. This does not, however, resolve the problem. Moving to a position whereby the public expenditure provides $D^{\dagger}$ of defense and $A^{\dagger}$ of aid may make the pro-food aid lobbyist more satisfied than at **D**, but only at the expense of the priorities of the strong defense group. Conversely, with the attainable position of $D^{\dagger\dagger}$ and $A^{\dagger\dagger}$, the pro-defense group is more satisfied than at **A** but the pro-food aid group is less satisfied. Just as there is no objective way of comparing points **D** and **A** on the possibility curve, there is no way of comparing intermediate combinations; it is a matter of judgment that, in practice, involves a set of secondary criteria.

Put another way, the current tangle of policy debates surrounding cargo preference and food aid stems from a fundamental flaw in the way the policy is perceived. Looking from a different perspective, Jan Tinbergen (1956) classified some economic quantities as targets and others as instruments. Targets are variables that policy-makers wish to influence, whereas the latter are variables that policy-makers can control directly. He emphasized that achieving the desired values of a certain number of targets requires the policy-maker to control at least an equal number of instruments. The problem regarding food aid is that essentially one instrument, namely cargo preference, is being used in trying to achieve at least two explicit targets (to provide food to populations in need and to maintain a mercantile marine for security reasons) and one less explicit target (that the maritime sector is protected from international competition in the carriage trade). This picture is made clear by Bageant et al. (2010), 'The most salient problem with the current formulation of the agricultural cargo preference program is the difficulty inherent to pursuing multiple policy objectives through a single policy instrument.'

The problem that can arise, and that Jan Tinbergen understood, is that the use of limited instruments relative to targets generally leads to conflicts, and with this ultimately to serious inefficiencies in trying to meet the targets. In Figure 8.3, in terms of cargo preference, it is often not just a matter of either being at **A** or **B**, but not even being on the production possibility line between them. For example, as active military involvement in Iraq and Afghanistan declined, so did the commercial maritime logistics capacity. This led to pressure for more use of US registered ships to carry food aid, although these were more costly than capacity on the open market, thus reducing funds available for food acquisition.

Additionally, security and aid policies can actually run counter to each other. It has been recognized since the days of the Marshall Plan that it is important for long-term political stability to give economic and humanitarian aid to those in need after a conflict – the title 'Food for Peace Program' has meaning! This, however, is at the very time when the pressures are to divert resources from aid to support a reserve fleet. This is not to say at all that a reserve fleet is not needed, but using cargo preference to support it leads to a reduction in the effectiveness of policies aimed at limiting conflicts.

There are also the questions of how targets are prioritized when insufficient instruments are not in play, and in this context, how George Stigler's (1971) concern that those supplying goods and services may 'capture' the policies. Maskin and Tirole (1990) set this within the principal–agent problem involving the ability of the principal, the government, to monitor and control its agents, the shipping companies. In the case of shipping food aid, the US maritime industry has a vested interest in carrying as much aid as possible in US registered ships and uses lobbying power and control over information to support its position. This captures the argument, and the principal is seldom well equipped to assess this.

One, albeit narrow, way of looking at the prioritization of measures is in terms of an external criterion, and in this case income and employment generation is often used. Fiscal multipliers are generally deployed for quantification. These macroeconomic concepts, designed to assess the consequences of major changes in fiscal policies of a nation, however, are more problematic when used at the micro level.

The underlying idea is that if there are underused resources in an economy, the government can step in and, by running a fiscal deficit, employ these resources. In turn the expenditure of this income by the newly employed will circulate, creating more jobs and output, with the additional income being spent leading to further spirals in employment and income. The fact that not all income will be spent in each round, that some will be kept back as savings, some will go to buy imports, and some will be taken in taxes, increasingly mutes the impact of the injection over the cycles. The outcome is a constrained overall increase in jobs and income but in excess of the initial multiplicand.

The macro concept, let alone those applied to industries, has come under a variety of criticisms. In particular, government fiscal injections have to be financed in some way other than through raising general taxes that would simply offset the multiplicand. Equally, borrowing on financial markets faces the problem that it can 'crowd-out' private investment and, as with taxation, set in motion a reverse multiplier. There are also issues about whether the magnitude of the 'leakages' from the multiplier is so large that it effectively reduces the magnitude of the income spiral to near zero. The size of the aggregate fiscal multiplier, which is also often used in industrial studies, has been the subject of considerable academic work that suggests it falls well below the estimates often mooted by politicians and lobbyists.[9]

At the meso-level when policy involves fiscal injections in particular industries rather than broadly across the economy, the multiplier has often been disaggregated following the advent of input–output analysis in the 1950s, although there has been considerable misuse of this.

Input–output analysis was designed to provide guidance on overall inputs required to produce a given output, including secondary inputs needed to provide the primary inputs. It addresses the question, according to its originator Wassily Leontief (1941), 'what level of output should each of the n industries in an economy produce, in order that it will just be sufficient to satisfy the total demand for that product?' Thus the input–output model makes it possible, under an extreme set of assumptions, to determine the output of each industry that must be produced to obtain a given amount for final demand. Its usefulness is in highlighting bottlenecks in supply that might arise and could stymie the ability to produce the target level of output. If there are inadequate inputs, outputs from elsewhere in the system need to be transferred in, with their own complex interactions throughout the economy, or the output target for the sector of interest must be revised down.

A major misuse of the technique involves reversing the logic of what input–output analysis was designed to do, and instead it is used to trace out across sectors the implications of fiscal injections into the system on levels of output. The original use relied upon numerous restrictive assumptions, not least of which is that there are no scale economies in production and that there is a fixed production technology implying that doubling output requires a doubling of all inputs. It is also assumed that there is a perfectly elastic supply of factors of production.

Despite these issues, the use of both multipliers and input–output at the meso-level has become widespread, and with this has been a tendency to have parameter inflation. A major problem in many policy comparisons is that the dispersion of overall gains from an action is estimated but the dispersion of costs across sectors is ignored. The point is made clear regarding maritime studies by Hercules Haralambides (1996):

> [E]stimates of the economic impacts of an industry are, with rare exceptions, measures of *gross*, not *net* impacts [italics in original]. A net impact would need to reflect all opportunities available elsewhere in the economy for the resources used directly by the industry and indirectly by all other industries. For example, if the demand for shipping were to decline and the services provided by the shipping industry were to decline, seafarers might remain employed in other maritime occupations or other industries. In this case, the provision of service by the merchant marine would not have resulted in a gain in national employment. Moreover, if the decline in service provided by the merchant marine did not affect the provision of port services and the production of other domestic goods and services because foreign-flag operators taking the place of national shipping operators would have used these goods and services, then the jobs associated with the provision of merchant marine service would not have been lost with the decline in service provided by the merchant marine. Hence, shipping would not have indirectly generated employment gains in other domestic industries.

There are also longer-term, often dynamic effects ignored in multiplier style work. For the coefficients of any input–output analysis to hold, there must be slack, unemployed resources available; and this must hold for each round of the multiplier spiral. Often an industrial policy designed to stimulate income or jobs in a particular sector such as shipping because slack is thought to exist there, ignores the fact that these unemployed factors will need to combine with factors taken from elsewhere where there is full employment (Coughlin and Mandelbaum, 2011). This sets in motion negative multipliers in industries from which these factors are drawn.

Perhaps the greatest potential for overestimating multiplier effects stems from their underlying assumption of a fixed technology (Button, 2012b). In practice there are market reactions and technical changes to consider if markets are manipulated. Any increase in the demands for the outputs of a sector will, unless all the resources were previously unused, lead to the price of inputs rising and efforts to reduce their use in production, either by substituting cheaper inputs from other sectors or by improving the technical efficiency of their use. The former will involve reduced outputs and higher prices for consumers in the sectors that lose their productive capacity, thus setting in train reverse multipliers.

As highlighted, the inherent danger of using multiplier and input–output measures in assessing the impact of any government expenditure, including that related to cargo preference, is that it almost inevitably leads to gross overestimations because of the double counting involved and/or the lack of netting out of costs. We briefly comment on the problems that are inherent in some of the work that has been conducted regarding the maritime sector.

Nathan Associates (1995) produced a general assessment of the economic outcomes of US federal aid to the merchant fleet and concluded, with no indications of its statistical significance, that the impact at the time was about 107 000 jobs and $4.5 billion in direct, indirect and induced effects. Nonetheless, Promar International (2010) proceeds to use this gross assessment input–output analysis approach using an extraordinarily high employment multiplier of 8.56 for the US maritime contribution to the movement of food aid. This is in a sector where a 49 percent foreign ownership of ships is allowed, with the remainder often being owned by a foreign subsidiary, meaning that any multiplicand is immediately reduced as parts of the profits are not retained in the US, and where up to 25 percent of the crew may be non-nationals or residents, thus leaking income overseas, where also most of the ships used are built, and where many inputs to the sector, fuel, victuals, and so on, are partly foreign sourced.

Elizabeth Bageant et al. (2010), in contrast, move towards a net approach in their analysis, focusing on the costs of the jobs created as a result of the cargo preference policy. They conclude that meeting cargo preference requirements costs taxpayers roughly $140 million, a premium of 46 percent over using the competitive freight market. Additionally, counter to cargo preference requirements, 70 percent of US-flag vessels eligible to carry food aid failed to qualify as militarily useful under MARAD criteria. The cost of maintaining a pool of roughly 1400 mariners on cargo preference vessels amounted to about $99 300 per mariner. However, as with most work in this field, there are no real indicators of the statistical significance of these results.

The exactitude of the calculations and their relevance to 2015 may be questioned, but the methodology adopted has merit to it in its simplicity and the openness of the discussion. An attempt to explicitly criticize, as opposed to evaluating, Bageant et al., USA Maritime (2010) focuses on data and factual issues, some not germane to the quantitative points made by Bageant et al., but it also comments on methodology. There is, for example, commentary on a neglected $10 billion in capital costs and $1 billion in annual costs savings to the US Transportation Command of the readiness initiatives, although this seems to relate to the entirety of the initiatives and not specifically to cargo preference. It also claims, using essentially gross multipliers, that cargo preference contributes $1.9 billion to the US economy and 33 000 jobs. Even if these very large figures were correct, they ignore the opportunity costs involved.

In Button (2015), I produced some back-of-the-envelope calculations – there was no pretense that the data, including that from official sources, had any exactitude about it – considering the implications of the US cargo preference returning to 75 percent from its current 50 percent. The numbers produced suggest that this greater use of US-flag carriers would at best result in an additional 298 US mariners being engaged at $13.5 million per annum; the system is one of continuous 'subsidies' for each maritime employee and not one of lump sums per worker, as is more common. One should for completeness include the possible employment added to the US shipbuilding industry, estimated at around 153 jobs if all the extra capacity was US built, as a result of the need for more US-flagged vessels.

Whether this is justified is largely a question of political economy in that there is as part of the arithmetic the need to assess the security benefits to the US of the 75 percent preference level against the loss of goodwill, and possibly heighted security concern, of not providing as much aid. Not something easily expressed in economic terms. But in addition to this there are the negative immediate impacts on the US economy of moving more aid on US-flagged ships.

Button (2015) only seeks to provide broad quantifications of these, but they include loss of at least 27 jobs in the agricultural sector as less food is grown in the US and a small loss of port jobs as less food aid is shipped. These are conservative estimates; for example, a US Department of Agriculture, Economic Research Service (2011) study found that $1 billion of agricultural exports supported 6800 American jobs in 2011, which translated, using the assumption regarding changes to food aid policy, to a reduction in US farm employment of 74.

These are tentative calculations, and there would be many other ripple effects that are not easily quantifiable; also, not all of the extra maritime workers will have been unemployed, and even if unemployed may be receiving a variety of state supports. In these cases, their employment in food aid shipping will have 'crowding out' effects elsewhere in the US economy setting off reverse income multipliers. This is true, irrespective of whether they were previously active in the maritime sector or any other industry. Some of the crews' income is also likely to be spent outside of the US when 'at sea'. In such cases this involves leakages that extend beyond those normally associated with import purchases. In a nutshell, the calculations of the impact of reforming cargo preference based on the need for a secure US maritime supply are complex, and higher than many have estimated.

8.7 CONCLUSIONS

The maritime sector because of its size and importance in international trade is in many ways a logical target for terrorist attacks and adverse commercial-based actions such as piracy. As a generalization, much of the attention to date regarding terrorism has been proactive, whereas that for piracy much more reactive. It has also been a transportation sector where there has been, at least in the US, considerable effort to coordinate and optimize the actions of the public and private sectors with multiple layers of institutional structures, both national and international, designed to provide protection.

Nevertheless, as with many areas of security, the private market has an inherent tendency to undersupply. This is in part because of potential free-rider problems – protection for a port or intermodal facility protects all users – but also the lack of complete property rights, and of de facto contracts, for the open sea means that large parts of the 'infrastructure' are essentially commons. Added to this, many terrorist acts, because of their infrequency, are more a matter of uncertainty than actuarial risk and this precludes the development of an effective private sector insurance market. Cargo interests, therefore, cannot be expected to carry the full cost of maritime container security. They do have an interest in ensuring that what is provided as a public good continues to also facilitate trade, albeit it a more secure manner. Hence it is not surprising that the focus of those interviewed across a range of quantitative studies is forward looking, with a greater concern for ensuring that if standards for electronic seals are introduced, for example, that they be not too prescriptive, that lines of communication between security officials and industry remain open and are effective, and that 'one size fits all' solutions are not imposed.[10]

A few shipping and rail companies have considerable power and influence through their own security programs. While concerns about chemical, biological, radiological or nuclear weapons in a box ('Trojan Horse' scenarios) drive current security measures from a government perspective, most companies agree that by the time the box arrives in the port, it is too late if the container is itself the weapon (or the ship the weapon). While they are generally supportive of measures that push back the border nearer to the source, the companies interviewed in the various studies cited in the chapter are much more concerned about incident management and remediation. This reflects something of a dichotomy of views between government and commerce that highlights their different constituents, the stakeholders and the stockholders, that is, as elsewhere, a key challenge to overcome in political economy.

NOTES

1. The privateers 'licensed' by the British crown during Elizabethan times epitomize what is often seen as state supported piracy.
2. For a discussion of this issue in the particular context of piracy in the Horn of Africa that has attracted considerable media coverage, besides inflicting commercial and other damage, see Sullivan (2010). For a discussion of the success rate of modern pirates see Psarros et al. (2011).
3. The 2013 movie *Captain Phillips* brought the issue home to a wider public.
4. The Code has two requirements that exceed the minimums in the ISPS Code. It requires the establishment of Transport Worker Identification Cards for domestic port personnel and that the US government not only assess the security plans of foreign ports, but also the effectiveness of a foreign nation's security oversight.
5. Similar programs include Canada's Partners in Protection Program.
6. As with the cargo preference system discussed here, the Jones (Merchant Marine) Act of 1920 provides security of supply of US coastal shipping by enforcing a legal monopoly use of US vessels. But this also brings any security it delivers at a price; see US International Trade Commission (1999).
7. Sixteen of the ships were built in South Korea; six in the US; five in Japan; three each in Germany, Portugal and Taiwan; and one each in China, Denmark, France and Norway. The US-built ships carried less than 6 percent of the food moved by the US flags, half were between 8 and 16 years old, and the others between 23 and 48 years.
8. Shipments are not large; for example those weighing between 10 and 560 tonnes accounted for 755 shipments, two-thirds of the total, but only represented 10 percent of the tonnage of food aid shipped. The next 10 percent by weight of shipments ranged between 560 and 1110 tonnes and accounted for 174 shipments. This can be contrasted to the 11 of 51 US-flagged ships used to carry food aid, all of which exceeded 60 000 dead-weight tonnes.
9. Valerie Ramey (2011) provides a summary, 'At this point it seems that the bulk of estimates imply that the aggregate multiplier for a temporary rise in government purchases not accompanied by an increase in current distortionary taxes is probably between 0.8 and 1.5.' Regarding the US, Owyang et al. (2013) conclude it is 'between 0.7 and 0.9', with it being higher during slack periods; the Canadian multiplier is found to be 0.5. At a more local, state level, looking at fiscal injections from pension changes, Shoag (2013) finds a multiplier of 1.43.
10. When electronic seals were proposed by the US Department of Homeland Security in 2002 as the 'frontline' technological solution to security, there was no subsequent agreement on standards and it was later concluded by the Department that the integrity of the seal does not guarantee that the contents of a container is as stated, thus it was decided to focus resources on cargo data and scanning technologies (Edmonson, 2006).

9. Some conclusions

It is better to be roughly right than precisely wrong
Carveth Read

The term *economics* comes from the Ancient Greek οἰκονομία (*oikonomia*, 'management of a household, administration') from οἶκος (*oikos*, 'house') + νόμος (*nomos*, 'custom' or 'law'), hence 'rules of the house(hold)'. Economics is thus essentially about rules and the choices that have to be made in defining and implementing these rules. Indeed, the idea of 'opportunity cost' lies at the root of most economic analysis. This in turn implies that everything has its price, and that, in today's parlance, there is no such thing as a free lunch. But put another way, given we have scarce resources, it implies that that there are limits governing how we can focus all our resources on one thing; the price just becomes too high after a while, and indeed may be infinite. Complete security is, therefore, more utopian than realism; but it does provide a target or a hypothetical benchmark. And this applies to transportation as much as any other activity.

The challenge of ensuring a socially acceptable secure transportation system, where its benefits exceed its costs, has been with us ever since man began to move about and to trade. The nature and dimensions of the problems encountered in attaining this socially acceptable level of security have obviously changed considerably over time, as have its details, and will inevitably evolve in the future. Equally, the public and private response to the security situation has shifted, not only as new challenges have emerged but also as new technologies and approaches have been developed, and as social preferences have changed. One reason we get so concerned about security issues today that in the past were treated almost as simple facts of life is the much higher income levels we enjoy, which make the costs of insecurity much greater.

What this implies is that while static analysis of the issues involved in increasing security can offer insights about security issues at any point in time, the shifting nature of the situation necessitates more dynamic analysis to handle the longer-term challenges of maintaining a reasonably secure social structure. And with this is a need for a reasonably secure transportation system.

While a lot of publicity has been focused on ongoing security issues, the situation today is probably, especially if account is taken of the number of people who travel and the volume of goods moved, objectively less serious than it has been at virtually any time in the past. The media attention brings vivid images of individual and multiple acts of terrorism before the general public in a novel and explicit way, often implicitly suggesting that attacks on transportation are increasing both in number and impact. But in aggregate, transportation is relatively secure. The problem is one of the extent to which economics can help the general public and policy-makers to understand the difference between what is thought to be happening and the actuality of the situation. Clearer expositions of the costs and benefits of protecting transportation would seem likely to be helpful in this regard.

The important issues for economists really revolve around the need to become more involved in security matters, and also to appreciate that for economics to be useful in this, and indeed other areas, economists need to accept that technically brilliant models have little utility unless they actually explain human behavior in a positive sense, or offer helpful policy assessments in a normative sense. As Thomas Piketty, author of the best-selling *Capital in the Twenty-First Century* (Piketty, 2014) put in a 2015 interview for the *Financial Times*, 'Too often, economists build very complex mathematical models to look scientific and impress people. I have nothing against mathematics – I initially trained as a mathematician – but it's usually to hide a lack of ideas.'

References

ABT Associates (2003) *The Economic Impact of Nuclear Terrorist Attacks on Freight Transport Systems in an Age of Seaport Vulnerability*, Contract # DTRS57-03-P-80130, US DOT/RSPA/Volpe Cambridge, MA: National Transportation Systems Center.

Akerlof, G.A. (1970) The market for 'lemons': quality uncertainty and the market mechanism, *Quarterly Journal of Economics*, 84, 488–500.

Akers, B. (2007) A better way than the Transportation Security Administration, *Christian Science Monitor*, 21 March.

Anderson, R. and Moore, T. (2006) The economics of information security, *Science*, 314, 610–13.

Anderson, T. (2006) Terror may be at bay at ports; shipping hubs too vulnerable, *The Daily News of Los Angeles*, 18 May.

Applebaum, A. (2005) Airport security's grand illusion, *Washington Post*, 15 June, A25.

Arrow, K.J. (1963) Uncertainty and welfare economics of medical care, *American Economic Review*, 53, 941–73.

Arrow, K.J. (1965) *Aspects of the Theory of Risk Bearing*, Helsinki: Yrgö Jahnssonin Säätio.

Australian Government Attorney-General's Department (2006) *Shopping Centres Risk Context Statement*, Canberra: Commonwealth of Australia.

Ayres, I. and Levitt, S.D. (1998) Measuring positive externalities from unobservable victim precaution: an empirical analysis of Lojack, *Quarterly Journal of Economics*, 113, 43–77.

Bageant, E.R., Barrett, C.B. and Lentz, E.C. (2010) Food aid and agricultural cargo preference, *Applied Economic Perspectives and Policy*, 4, 624–41.

Baker, T.A., Connaughton, D., Zhang, J.J. and Spengler, J.O. (2007) Perceived risk of terrorism and related risk management practices of NCAA Division IA football stadium managers, *Journal of Legal Aspects of Sport*, 13, 145–79.

Baumol, W.J., Litan, R.E. and Schramm, C.J. (2007) *Good Capitalism, Bad Capitalism and the Economics of Growth and Prosperity*, New Haven, CT: Yale University Press.

Baumol, W.J., Panzar, J.C. and Willig, R.D. (1982) *Contestable Markets*

and the Theory of Industry Structure, New York: Harcourt Brace Jovanovich.
Becker, G. (1968) Crime and punishment: an economic approach, *Journal of Political Economy*, 76, 169–217.
Bede (741) *Historia Ecclesiastica Gentis Anglorum*, Monkwearmouth.
Bellish, J. (2013) *The Economic Cost of Somali Piracy, 2012*, Working Paper, Denver, CO: One Earth Future Foundation.
Bichou, K. (2014) Risks and costs of maritime security: review and analysis, in K. Bichou, J.S. Szyliowicz and L. Zamparini (eds) *Maritime Transport Security: Issues, Challenges and National Policies*, Cheltenham, UK and Northampton, MA, USA: Edward Elgar Publishing.
Blalock, G., Kadiyali, V. and Simon, D.H. (2007) The impact of post-9/11 airport security measures on the demand for air travel, *Journal of Law and Economics*, 50, 731–55.
Blunk, S.S., Clark, D.E. and McGibany, J.M. (2006) Evaluating the long-run impacts of the September 11th terrorist attacks on US domestic airline travel, *Applied Economics*, 38, 363–70.
Booz Allen Hamilton (2003) *Port Security War Game: Implications for US Supply Chains*, New York: Booz Allen Hamilton.
Bowden, A. and Basnet, S. (2012) *The Economic Cost of Somali Piracy, 2011*, Working Paper, Denver, CO: One Earth Future Foundation.
Brooks, M.R. and Button, K.J. (2006) Market structure and shipping security, *Maritime Economics and Logistics*, 8, 100–120.
Brooks, M.R. and Button, K.J. (2007) Maritime container security: a cargo interest perspective, in K. Bichou, M. Bell and A. Evans (eds) *Risk Management in Port Operations, Logistics and Supply Chain Security*, London: Informa.
Brown, B. (2006) C-TPAT: security compliance loan program, *Exportwise*, Spring, 6–7.
Button, K.J. (2005) Shipping economics: where we are and looking ahead from an institutional economics perspective, *Maritime Policy and Management*, 32, 39–58.
Button, K.J. (2008) The economics of shopping mall security, *Journal of Transportation Security*, 1, 127–39.
Button, K.J. (2012a) The economics of meeting the challenges of air transportation security, *Aviation and Space Journal*, 11, 2–17.
Button, K.J. (2012b) What do we know about the multiplier effects of regional transportation infrastructure on regional economies? Some reflections, *Studies in Regional Science*, 42, 61–75.
Button, K.J. (2015) The political economy of shipping US food aid under the Cargo Preference regime, *Maritime Economics and Logistics* (forthcoming).

Button, K.J. (2016) Public–private partnerships: a survey of economic considerations, *Transportation Planning and Technology* (forthcoming).

Button, K.J. and Pels, E. (2010) International air transport: the impact of globalization on activity levels, in *Globalisation, Transport and the Environment*, Paris: OECD.

Button, K.J., Stough, R. and Thibault, M. (2003) Securing the logistics of the shopping mall, in E. Taniguchi and R.G. Thompson (eds) *Recent Advances in City Logistics*, Oxford: Elsevier.

Campaniello, N. (2012) Mega events in sports and crime: evidence from the 1990 football World Cup, *Journal of Sports Economics*, 14, 148–70.

Cauley, J. and Iksoon Im, E. (1988) Intervention policy analysis of skyjackings and other terrorist incidents, *American Economic Review, Papers and Proceedings*, 78, 27–31.

Chen, B.R. and Chiu, Y.S. (2010) Public–private partnerships: task interdependence and contractibility, *International Journal of Industrial Organization*, 28, 591–603.

Coase, R.H. (1937) The nature of the firm, *Economica*, 4, 386–405.

Coase, R.H. (1960) The problem of social cost, *Journal of Law and Economics*, 3, 1–40.

Coase, R.H. (1992) The institutional structure of production, *American Economic Review*, 82, 713–19.

Containerisation International (2006) *Containerisation International Yearbook 2006*, London: Containerisation International.

Cooper, M.C., Lambert, D.M. and Pagh, J. (1997) Supply chain management: More than a new name for logistics, *International Journal of Logistics Management*, 8, 1–14.

Coughlin, C.C. and Mandelbaum, T.B. (2011) A consumer's guide to regional economic multipliers, *Federal Reserve Bank of St. Louis Review*, 73, 19–32.

Coughlin, C.C., Cohen, J.P. and Khan, S.R. (2002) Aviation security and terrorism: a review of the economic issues, *Federal Bank of St. Louis Review*, September/October, 9–24.

Davis, R.C., Ortiz, C., Rowe, R., Broz, J., Rigakos, G. and Collins, P. (2006) *An Assessment of the Preparedness of Large Retail Malls to Prevent and Respond to Terrorist Attack*, US Department of Justice Document 216641, Washington, DC.

De Waard, J. (1999) The private security industry in an international perspective, *European Journal of Criminology Policy and Research*, 7, 143–74.

Demsetz, H. (1968) Why regulate utilities? *Journal of Law and Economics*, 11, 55–65.

Economides, N. (1996) The economics of networks, *International Journal of Industrial Organisation*, 14, 673–99.
Edgeworth, F.Y. (1881) *Mathematical Physics*, London: Kegan Paul.
Edmonson, R.G. (2006) On the back burner, *The Journal of Commerce*, 14 August, 19.
Eggers, W. (2005) *Prospering in the Secure Economy*, New York: Deloitte.
Ehrlich, I. and Becker, G.S. (1972) Market insurance, self-insurance, and self-protection, *Journal of Political Economy*, 80, 623–48.
Endorf, C.E. (2004) Outsourcing security: the need, the risk, the providers, and the process, *Information Systems Security*, 12, 17–23.
Erman, M. (2002) Mall security still too relaxed, *The Charlotte Observer*, November.
European Commission (2006) *Communication from the Commission of 12 December 2006 on a European Programme for Critical Infrastructure Protection*, EU COM(2006) 786 final, Brussels.
European Conference of Ministers of Transport (2004) *Security in Transport: Report on Container Transport Security Across Modes* (CEMT/CM(2004)22), Paris: European Conference of Ministers of Transport.
Flynn, S.E. (2004) *America the Vulnerable: How our Government is Failing to Protect us from Terrorism*, New York: HarperCollins Publishers in cooperation with the Council on Foreign Relations.
Frey, B.S. (2009) How can business cope with terrorism? *Journal of Policy Modeling*, 31, 779–87.
Frey, B.S. and Luechinger, S. (2003) How to fight terrorism: alternatives to deterrence, *Defence and Peace Economics*, 14, 237–49.
Furubotn, E.G. and Richter, R. (1997) *Institutions and Economic Theory*, Ann Arbor, MI: University of Michigan Press.
Gang, L., Hollinger, R.C. and Dabney, D.A. (1999) The relationship between crime and private security at US shopping centers, *American Journal of Criminal Justice*, 23, 601–21.
Garner, A.A. (2002) Consumer confidence after September 11, *Economic Review, Federal Reserve Bank of Kansas City*, 87(2), 5–26.
Garreau, J. (1991) *Edge City: Life on the New Frontier*, New York: Doubleday & Company.
Gkritza, K., Niemeier, D. and Mannering, F. (2006) Airport security screening and changing passenger satisfaction: an exploratory assessment, *Journal of Air Transport Management*, 12, 213–19.
Glaeser, E.L. and Shapiro, J.M. (2002) Cities and warfare: the impact of terrorism on urban form, *Journal of Urban Economics*, 51, 205–24.
Gordon, P., Moore, J.E. and Richardson, H.W. (2009) Economic impact analysis of terrorism events: recent methodological advances and

findings, in *Terrorism and International Transport: Towards a Risk-based Security Policy*, Paris: OECD.

Gordon, P., Moore, J.E., Richardson, H.W. and Pan, Q. (2006) The costs of a terrorist attack on terminal island at the twin ports of Los Angeles and Long Beach, in J.D. Haveman and H.J. Shatz (eds) *Protecting the Nation's Seaports: Balancing Security and Cost*, San Francisco: Public Policy Institute of California.

Gorman, S.P. (2005) *Networks, Security, and Complexity: The Role of Public Policy in Critical Infrastructure Protection*, Cheltenham, UK and Northampton, MA, USA: Edward Elgar Publishing.

Gould, J.E., Macharis, C. and Haasis, H.D. (2010) Emergence of security in supply chain management literature, *Journal of Transport Security*, 3, 287–302.

Guasch, J.L., Laffont, J-J. and Straub, S. (2008) Renegotiation of concession contracts in Latin America: evidence from the water and transport sectors, *International Journal of Industrial Organization*, 26, 421–42.

Hall, M. (2003) Private security guards: homeland defense's weak link, *USA Today*, 23 January, A.01.

Hancock, K.L. (2001) Hazardous goods, in A.M. Brewer et al. (eds) *Handbook of Logistics and Supply-chain Management*, Oxford: Pergamon.

Haralambides, H.E. (1996) The economic impact of shipping on the national economy, paper presented at the International Conference on Shipping, Ports and Logistics Services: Solutions for Global Issues. The International Association of Maritime Economists, 26–28 June, Vancouver.

Hardy, C. (2007) Shopping malls – possible terrorist targets? *CIP Report*, April, 5–7.

Hart, O. (2008) Reference points and the theory of the firm, *Economica*, 75, 404–11.

Hart, O. and Moore, J. (1988) Incomplete contracts and renegotiation, *Econometrica*, 56, 755–85.

Hart, O., Sheifer, A. and Vishy, R. (1997) The proper scope of government: theory and an application to prisons, *Quarterly Journal of Economics*, 111, 1127–62.

Heal, G. and Kunreuther, H. (2005) IDS models of airline security, *Journal of Conflict Resolution*, 49, 201–17.

Heaver, T.D. (1973) A theory of shipping conference pricing and policies, *Maritime Studies and Management*, 1, 17–30.

Helferich, O.K. and Cook, R.L. (2002) *Securing the Supply Chain*, Oak Brook: Council of Logistics Management.

Hendricks, K.B. and Singhal, V.R. (2005) Association between supply

chain glitches and operating performance, *Management Science*, 51, 695–711.
Holcombe, R.G. (1997) A theory of the theory of public goods, *Review of Austrian Economics*, 10, 1–22.
Hollingsworth, J.R. and Boyer, R. (1997) *Contemporary Capitalism*, Cambridge: Cambridge University Press.
Hoppe, H.H. (1989) Falacies of the public goods theory and the production of security, *Journal of Libertarian Studies*, 9, 27–42.
International Maritime Organization (2002a) *FAQ on ISPS Code and Maritime Security*, London: IMO.
International Maritime Organization (2002b) *The Safety of Life at Sea, 1974, As Amended Mandatory Requirements Regarding the Provisions of Chapter XI-2 of the International Convention For the Safety of Life At Sea, 1974, As Amended*, London: IMO.
Ito, H. and Lee, D. (2005) Assessing the impact of the September 11 terrorist attacks on US airline demand, *Journal of Economics and Business*, 57, 75–95.
Kanafani, A. and Huang, J. (2010) Securing linked transportation systems: economic implications and investment strategies, *Journal of Transport Security*, 3, 257–74.
Kaplan, E. (2009) Targets for terrorists: post-9/11 aviation security, available at http://www.cfr.org/publication/11397/targets_for_terrorists.html.
Kasarda, J.D., Green, J. and Sullivan, D. (2004) *Air Cargo: Engine of Economic Development, Center for Air Commerce*, Chapel Hill, NC: University of North Carolina at Chapel Hill.
Knight, F.H. (1921) *Risk, Uncertainty and Profit*, New York: Houghton Mifflin.
Kumar, S. and Verruso, J. (2008) Risk assessment for the security of inbound containers at US ports: a failure, mode, effects, and criticality analysis approach, *Transportation Journal*, 47, 26–41.
Laffont, J-J. and Tirole, J. (1993) *A Theory of Incentives in Procurement and Regulation*, Cambridge, MA: MIT Press.
Lancaster, K.J. (1966) A new approach to consumer theory, *Journal of Political Economy*, 74, 132–57.
Landes, W.M. (1978) An economic study of US aircraft hijacking, *Journal of Law and Economics*, 21, 1–31.
Lane, F. (1966) The economic meaning of war and protection, in *Venice and History: the Collected Papers of Frederic C. Lane*, Baltimore, MD: Johns Hopkins Press.
LaTourrette, T., Howell, D.R., Mosher, D.E. and MacDonald, J. (2006) *Reducing Terrorism Risk at Shopping Centers: An Analysis of Potential Security Options*, Santa Monica, CA: RAND Corporation.

Leibenstein, H. (1979) A branch of economics is missing: micro-micro theory, *Journal of Economic Literature*, 17, 477–502.
Leontief, W. (1941) *The Structure of American Economy, 1919–1929*, Cambridge, MA: Harvard University Press.
Leruth, L.E. (2012) Public–private cooperation in infrastructure development: a principal–agent story of contingent liabilities, fiscal risk, and other (un)pleasant surprises, *Network and Spatial Economics*, 12, 223–37.
Lewis, I. (1998) The Civil Reserve Air Fleet: balancing risks and incentives, *Transportation Journal*, 38, 32–40.
Li, S., Tallman, S.B. and Ferreira, M.P. (2005) Developing the eclectic paradigm as a model of global strategy: an application to the impact of the Sep.11 terrorist attacks on MNE performance levels, *Journal of International Management*, 11, 479–96.
Litan, R. and Orszag, P. (2002) A complicated intersection: public action to protect private property, *Brookings Review*, 20, 20–24.
Lohse, T., Robledo, J.R. and Schmidt, U. (2012) Self-insurance and self-protection as public goods, *Journal of Risk and Insurance*, 57–76.
Luzadder, D. (2006) Airports, tech firms in holding pattern on new security systems, *Travel Weekly*, 8 November.
Marshall, A. (1890) *Principles of Economics*, London: Macmillan.
Maskin, E. and Tirole, J. (1990) The principal–agent relationship with an informed principal: the case of private values, *Econometrica*, 58, 379–409.
Michael, R.T. and Becker, G.S. (1973) On the new theory of consumer behavior, *Swedish Journal of Economics*, 75, 378–96.
Morral, A.R., Price, C.C., Ortiz, D.S., Wilson, B., LaTourrette, T., Mobley, B.W., McKay, S. and Willis, H.H. (2012) *Modeling Terrorism Risk to the Air Transportation System An Independent Assessment of TSA's Risk Management Analysis Tool and Associated Methods*, Santa Monica, CA: RAND Corporation.
Mueller, D.C. (2003) *Public Choice III*, Cambridge: Cambridge University Press.
Mueller, J. (2004) A false sense of security, *Regulation*, 37, 42–6.
Mueller, J. and Stewart, M.G. (2010) Hardly existential: thinking rationally about terrorism, *Foreign Affairs*, 2 April, 1–5.
Nathan Associates (1995) *Economic Analysis of Federal Support for the Private Merchant Marine*, Washington, DC: American Maritime Congress.
North, D.C. (1994) Economic performance through time, *American Economic Review*, 84, 359–68.
O'Hanlon, M.E., Orszag, P.R., Daalder, I.H., Destler, I.M., Gunter, D.L.,

Litan, R.E. and Steinberg, J.E. (2002) *Protecting the American Homeland: A Preliminary Analysis*, Washington, DC: Brookings Institution.

Organisation for Economic Co-operation and Development (1992) *Market and Government Failures in Environmental Policy: The Case of Transport*, Paris: OECD.

Organisation for Economic Co-operation and Development (2003) *Security in Maritime Transport: Risk Factors and Economic Impact*, Paris: OECD.

Oster, C.V. and Strong, J.S. (2008) A review of Transportation Security Administration funding 2001–2007, *Journal of Transportation Security*, 1, 37–43.

Overstreet, J. and Clodfelter, R. (1995) Safety and security concerns of shopping center customers and the effect of these concerns on shopping behavior, *Journal of Shopping Center Research*, 2, 91–109.

Owyang, M.T., Ramey, V.A. and Zubairy, S. (2013) Are government spending multipliers greater during periods of slack? Evidence from twentieth-century historical data, *American Economic Review, Papers and Proceedings*, 103, 129–34.

Parry, A. (1976) *Terrorism from Robespierre*, New York: Vanguard Press.

Pigou, A. (1920) *The Economics of Welfare*, London: Macmillan.

Piketty, T. (2014) *Capital in the Twenty-First Century*, Cambridge, MA: Belknap Press.

Porter, M.E. (1985) *Competitive Advantage: Creating and Sustaining Superior Performance*, New York: Free Press.

Prentice, B. and Hickson, A. (2007) Benefits of security measures on transportation, *Journal of Transport Security*, 1, 3–14.

Prest, A.R. and Turvey, R. (1965) Cost–benefit analysis – a survey, *Economic Journal*, 75, 683–735.

Priks, M. (2015) The effects of surveillance cameras on crime: evidence from the Stockholm subway, *Economic Journal*, 125, F289–F305.

Promar International (2010) Impacts on the US economy of shipping international food aid: a report prepared for USA Maritime, Alexandria, VA: Promar International.

Psarros, G.D., Christianson, A.F., Skjong, R. and Gravir, G. (2011) On the success rates of maritime piracy attacks, *Journal of Transport Security*, 4, 309–35.

Ramey, V.A. (2011) Can government purchases stimulate the economy? *Journal of Economic Literature*, 49, 673–85.

Ramsey, F.P. (1931) *The Foundations of Mathematics and other Logical Essays*, London: Kegan Paul, Trend, Trubner and Co.

Record, J. (2003) *Bounding the Global War on Terrorism*, Carlisle: Strategic Studies Institute.

Romano, E. (1994) Making shopping centres safer, *Journal of Property Management*, 59, 46–51.
Rossiter, A. and Dresner, M. (2004) The impact of the September 11th security fee and passenger wait time on traffic diversion and highway fatalities, *Journal of Air Transport Management*, 10, 227–32.
Samuelson, P.A. (1954) The pure theory of public expenditures, *Review of Economics and Statistics*, 36, 350–56.
Schmid, A.P. and Jongman, A.J. (1988) *Political Terrorism: A New Guide to Actors, Authors, Concepts*, New Brunswick, NJ: Transaction Books.
Seidenstat, P. (2004) Terrorism, airport security, and the private sector, *Review of Policy Research*, 21, 275–91.
Shoag, D. (2013) Using state pension shocks to estimate fiscal multipliers since the Great Recession, *American Economic Review, Papers and Proceedings*, 103, 121–24.
Simon, H. (1955) A behavioral model of rational choice, *Quarterly Journal of Economics*, 69, 99–118.
SITPRO (2005) *Summary Notes from the Meeting of the 8th SITPRO Security Forum*, 20 April, available at http://www.sitpro.org.uk/policy/security/secfor8.html, accessed 10 August 2006.
Sly, O. (2001) *The Economics of Network Industries*, Cambridge: Cambridge University Press.
Smith, D. (2005) Prepared for the worst: malls improve technology and interaction with government authorities to deter terrorist attacks, *Shopping Centers Today*, November, available at http://www.icsc.org/srch/sct/sct1105/feat_security_prepared.php.
Stewart, M.G. and Mueller, J. (2008) A risk and cost–benefit assessment of United States aviation security measures, *Journal of Transportation Security*, 1, 143–59.
Stewart, M.G. and Mueller, J. (2014) Cost–benefit analysis of airport security: are airports too safe? *Journal of Air Transport Management*, 19–28.
Stigler, G.J. (1971) The theory of economic regulation, *Bell Journal of Economics and Management Science*, 3, 3–18.
Stiglitz, J.E. and Rothschild, M.E. (1976) Equilibrium in competitive insurance markets, *Quarterly Journal of Economics*, 90, 629–49.
Stross, R. (2006) Theatre of the absurd at the Transportation Security Administration, *New York Times*, 17 December, 5.
Subcommittee on Coast Guard and Maritime Transportation, US House of Representatives (2010) *Hearing on the 'Status of US-flagged Vessels in US-Foreign Trade'*, Washington, DC.
Sullivan, A.K. (2010) Piracy in the horn of Africa and its effects on the global supply chain, *Journal of Transport Security*, 3, 231–43.

Talas, R. and Menachof, D. (2014) Maritime terrorist attacks against seaports 1968–2007, in K. Bichou, J.S. Szyliowicz and L. Zamparini (eds) *Maritime Transport Security: Issues, Challenges and National Policies*, Cheltenham, UK and Northampton, MA, USA: Edward Elgar Publishing.

Thibault, M., Brooks, M.S. and Button, K.J. (2006) The response of the US maritime industry to the new container security initiatives, *Transportation Journal*, 45, 5–15.

Tiebout, C.M. (1956) A pure theory of local expenditures, *Journal of Political Economy*, 64, 416–24.

Tinbergen, J. (1956) *Economic Policy: Principles and Design*, Amsterdam: North-Holland.

Transportation Research Board (2003) *Cybersecurity of Freight Information Systems: A Scoping Study*, Transportation Research Board Special Report 274, Washington, DC.

US Department of Agriculture, Economic Research Service (2011) *Effects of Trade on the US Economy, 2011 Data Overview*, updated 17 June 2013, available at http://www.ers.usda.gov/data-products/agricultural-trade-multipliers/effects-of-trade-on-the-us-economy.aspx.

US Department of Transportation, Bureau of Transportation Statistics (2010) *United States (2007) Hazardous Materials, 2007 Economic Census, Transportation, 2007 Commodity Flow Survey*, Washington, DC: USDOT.

US Government Accountability Office (2004) *Homeland Security: Summary of Challenges Faced in Targeting Oceangoing Cargo Containers for Inspection*, GAO-04-557T, Washington, DC: GAO.

US Government Accountability Office (2005) *Aviation Fees: Review of Air Carriers' Year 2000 Passenger and Property Screening Costs*, April, Washington, DC.

US Government Accountability Office (2008) *TSA has Developed a Risk-based Covert Testing Program, but Could Better Mitigate Aviation Security Vulnerabilities Identified Through Covert Tests*, GAO-08-958, Washington, DC.

US Government Accountability Office (2009) *Aviation Security: TSA's Cost and Performance Study of Private-Sector Airport Screening*, GAO-09-27R, Washington, DC.

US House Committee on Transportation and Infrastructure (2011) *TSA Ignores More Cost-Effective Screening Model*, Washington, DC.

US International Trade Commission (1999) *The Economic Effects of Significant U.S. Import Restraints*, International Trade Commission, Washington, DC.

US Maritime Administration (2011) *Comparison of US and Foreign Flagged Operating Costs*, Washington, DC.

USA Martime (2010) *A Critical Analysis of 'Food Aid and Agricultural Cargo Preference'*, USA Maritime, Washington, DC.

Van Drake, S. (2001) Mall security moves beyond shoplifting, *The Business Journal*, November, 16.

Varian, H. (2004) System reliability and free riding, *Economics of Information Security*, 12, 1–15.

Vining, A.R., Boardman, A.E. and Poschmann, F. (2005) Public–private partnerships in the US and Canada: 'there are no free lunches', *Journal of Comparative Policy Analysis: Research and Practice*, 7, 199–220.

Waters, W.G. and Yu, C. (2003) Air security fees and highway safety, Proceedings of the 38th Canadian Transportation Research Forum Annual Conference.

Williamson, O.E. (1985) *The Economic Institutions of Capitalism*, New York: Free Press.

Williamson, O.E. (2000) The New Institutional Economics: taking stock, looking ahead, *Journal of Economic Literature*, 38, 595–613.

Williamson, O.E. (2008) Outsourcing: transactions cost economics and supply chain management, *Journal of Supply Chain Management*, 44, 5–16.

Willis, H.H. and Ortiz, D.S. (2004) *Evaluating the Security of the Global Supply Chain*, Arlington, TX: RAND Corporation.

Winston, C. (2006) *Government Failure versus Market Failure*, Washington, DC: Brookings Institution.

World Customs Organization (2002) *Resolution of the Customs Co-operation Council on Security and Facilitation of the International Trade Supply Chain*, June, available at http://www.wcoomd.org/ie/En/en.html.

World Customs Organization (2005) *Framework of Standards to Facilitate and Secure Global Trade*, June, available at http://www.wcoomd.org/ie/En/en.html.

World Shipping Council, the International Mass Retail Association, and the National Industrial Transportation League (2003) *In-transit Container Security Enhancement* (Working Paper), 9 September, available at http://www.retail-leaders.org.

Ybarra, S. (2013) *Overhauling US Airport Security*, Policy Brief 109, Washington, DC: Reason Foundation.

Index